g to

PIECES

w i t h o u t

FALLING

a p a r t

'This book is an original, provocative, and wonderful manual of transformation. With heartfelt warmth and a clear understanding of the mind, it offers a vision of who we are, who we think we are, and who we might become if we truly loved ourselves and all of life.'

SHARON SALZBERG, author of Lovingkindness: The Revolutionary Art of Happiness and A Heart as Wide as the World: Living with Mindfulness, Wisdom, and Compassion

'Mark Epstein's deep commitment to the practices of Buddhist meditation and psychotherapy is revealed in his rare capacity to weave between these traditions. Moving effortlessly from the analyst's couch to the meditator's cushion, *Going to Pieces Without Falling Apart* is an insightful and heartfelt exploration into the dilemma and joy of being human.'

STEPHEN BACHELOR, author of Buddhism Without Beliefs

'This is good reading – clear, warm, precise, full of poignant stories that hit home. I found it ever helpful.'

NATALIE GOLDBERG, author of Writing Down the Bones and Living Color: A Writer Paints Her World

going to

PIECES

without

FALLING

a p a r t

a buddhist perspective on wholeness

MARK EPSTEIN, M.D.

Thorsons
An Imprint of HarperCollins*Publishers*

Thorsons
An Imprint of HarperCollins*Publishers*
77–85 Fulham Palace Road,
Hammersmith, London W6 8JB

First published by Broadway Books, a division
of Bantam Doubleday Dell Publishing Group Inc.,
1540 Broadway, New York, NY 10036, USA
This edition by Thorsons 1999

10 9 8 7 6 5 4

A catalogue record for this book
is available from the British Library

ISBN 0 7225 3794 8

Printed in Great Britain by
Creative Print & Design (Wales), Ebbw Vale

for arlene

ALSO BY THE AUTHOR

Thoughts Without a Thinker

Men are afraid to forget their minds, fearing to fall through the Void with nothing to stay their fall. They do not know that the Void is not really void, but the realm of the real Dharma.

HUANG PO

CONTENTS

Acknowledgments xi

Introduction xv

part one LOOKING *starting where you are* 1

1. emptiness 3

2. surrender 29

part two SMILING *finding a practice* 49

3. meditation 51

4. connection 73

part three EMBRACING *releasing your heart* 93

5. tolerance 95

6. relationship 117

part four ORGASM *bringing it all back home* 137

7. passion 139

8. relief 159

Notes 183

Index 191

ACKNOWLEDGMENTS

I would like to thank all of my patients who have shared their lives, thoughts, and feelings with me as I have constructed this book. Their willingness to enter into dialogue and to range far afield of their own immediate concerns has been a source of continuing inspiration and exhilaration for me. I developed this book in collaboration with them and am grateful for the opportunity they have given me.

I would also like to thank a number of people whose conversations have sparked ideas that have found their way into this work: Michael Eigen, for thoughts on unintegration, Jeffrey Hopkins on sexual tantra, Stephen Batchelor on emptiness and imagination, Manny Ghent on surrender and aggression, Helen Tworkov on emotions in Buddhism, Joseph Goldstein and Sharon Salzberg on practice, Kiki Smith on writing and speaking, Wes Nisker on the four foundations of mindfulness, Jack Kornfield on relationships and the Dharma, Richard Kohn on the goddesses at the doorway, Daniel Goleman on the whole process of making a book that works, Robbie Stein on fear of breakdown, Jack Engler on mourning, and Michael Vincent Miller on disappointment and empathy. I owe particular thanks to Adam Phillips, from whose inspired writings on the British analyst D. W. Winnicott I appropriated my title.

Anne Edelstein, my literary agent, meticulously steered this project through sometimes rocky waters, and Janet Goldstein, Daisy Alpert, Charles Conrad, and William Shinker at Broadway Books saw fit to give their time and energy to making it come to be. George Lange took great pictures and continues to teach me about play.

My children, Sonia and Will, have discussed many aspects of this book with me since its (and their) inception and have done a great job of giving me support and showing me their pride in my endeavors. My wife Arlene, who has made the Dharma come alive for me and been my equal partner in ways that suffuse and transcend this particular book, has helped develop all of the major ideas in this work. I thank her for her innumerable contributions and for the hours of conversation that we have enjoyed. My parents, Frank and Sherrie, have been wonderfully supportive and interested throughout this process and have shared in its execution from start to finish.

Acknowledgments

My in-laws, Jean and Dave, have encouraged my writing from the beginning, and our babysitter and friend, Sheila Mangyal, has made all of this possible.

Except in the case of well-known figures introduced by first and last names, I have changed names and other identifying details or constructed composites in order to protect privacy.

INTRODUCTION

In the Zen tradition of Buddhism there is a story of a smart and eager university professor who comes to an old Zen master for teachings. The Zen master offers him tea and upon the man's acceptance he pours the tea into the cup until it overflows. As the professor politely expresses his dismay at the overflowing cup, the Zen master keeps on pouring.

"A mind that is already full cannot take in anything new," the master explains. "Like this cup, you are full of opinions and preconceptions." In order to find happiness, he teaches his disciple, he must first empty his cup.[1]

The central premise of this book is that the Western psychological notion of what it means to have a self is flawed. We are all trained to approach life like the professor in the story, filling ourselves up the way the master filled the cup with tea. Afflicted, as we are, with a kind of psychological materialism, we are concerned primarily with beefing ourselves up. Self-development, self-esteem, self-confidence, self-expression, self-awareness, and self-control are our most sought after attributes. But Buddhism teaches us that happiness does not come from any kind of acquisitiveness, be it material or psychological. Happiness comes from letting go. In Buddhism, the impenetrable, separate, and individuated self is more of the problem than the solution.

One of my first teachings about the limitations of the self came during my freshman year at Harvard. My first roommate there was a young man from the South named Steve who was the hardest worker I had ever seen. Steve spent every waking moment, and an increasing number of what should have been sleeping moments, studying for the five hardest courses that a freshman could take. As the semester wore on, Steve stopped bathing, going out for meals, and playing his guitar, while becoming increasingly obsessed with mastering every detail of economics, philosophy, and so on. He was intent on becoming the embodiment of what he imagined a successful Harvard freshman to be.

On his way to his first final exam, Steve slipped on the concrete stairs of our dorm and slid down several flights, knocking himself out. When he awoke, he had amnesia for the entire semester: He could remember only the first week of school and going home for Christmas. His memory for that semester of work never came back. He took the rest of the year off and returned the following year, chastened, to begin anew.

Steve went to pieces *and* fell apart. If he could have permitted himself more of the former, he might have escaped the intensity of the latter. Yet Steve's predicament typified all of ours that year. We all felt that we had to strive to consolidate our egos, to master our insecurities, and to become as "together" as the next person was. Steve merely went at it with more zeal than the rest of us could stomach. Just as the full cup could not hold any more tea, so too Steve could not contain all of the knowledge, information, and psychological attributes that he was attempting to swallow. What he needed instead was some recognition of his capacity to relax the grip of his ego and to empty his mind.

A few years after witnessing Steve's collapse, I heard the Dalai Lama speak for the first time on his first visit to the United States.

"All beings are seeking happiness," he said. "It is the purpose of life."

When I heard him say this, I remember scoffing at the idea. Something about it sounded so simplistic. But after I heard him say it eight or nine more times over the next few years, I started to pay attention to his actual meaning. He was addressing this idea of psychological materialism and the search for happiness through the acquisition of things, experiences, and beliefs. When we seek happiness through accumulation, either outside of ourselves—from other people, relationships, or material goods—or from our own self-development, we are missing the essential point. In either case we are trying to find completion. But according to Buddhism, such a strategy is doomed. Completion comes not from adding another piece to ourselves but from surrendering our ideas of perfection.

My roommate's experience was a metaphor for the limitations of self-development. Cramming himself full of the imagined constituents of a self, Steve succeeded only in knocking himself out. He could never be the perfect person he was trying to be. Unless he, and we, learn the lessons that Harvard was not teaching that year (how to lose ourselves, surrender control, or go to pieces without disintegrating), we will never be happy.

While psychotherapy has a long tradition of encouraging the development of a strong sense of self, Buddhism has an even longer tradition of teaching the value of collapsing that self. Part of my attraction to Buddhist meditation lies in this difference. Many of us come to therapy—and to psychological self-improvement in general—feeling that we are having trouble letting ourselves go: We are blocked creatively or emotionally, we have trouble falling asleep or having satisfying sex, or we suffer from feelings of isolation or alienation. Often we are afraid of falling apart, but the problem is that we have not learned how to give up control of ourselves. The traditional view of therapy as building up the self simply does not do justice to what we actually seek from the therapeutic process. We are looking for a way to feel more real, but we do not realize that to feel more real we have to push ourselves further into the unknown.

Buddhism has always made the self's ability to relax its boundaries the centerpiece of its teachings. It recognizes that the central issues of our lives, from falling in love to facing death, require an ability to surrender that often eludes us. Psychotherapy, through its analysis of childhood, has tended to turn us in a reflective direction, searching for the causes of unhappiness in an attempt to break free from the traumas of the past. Too often, though, it degenerates into finding someone to blame for our suffering. But within psychotherapy lies the potential for an approach that is compatible with Buddhist understanding, one in which the therapist, like the Zen master, can aid in making space in the mind.

People who know that I practice Buddhism as well as psychiatry are often surprised or disappointed to find that I do not promote some kind of hybrid "Buddhist" therapy. They want to know if I meditate together with my patients or if I teach them special techniques or spiritual disciplines. I tell them that this is mostly unnecessary. I like to quote the famous phrase of Sándor Ferenczi, the Hungarian psychoanalyst who was one of Freud's most intimate disciples. "The patient is not cured by free-associating," Ferenczi asserted, "he is cured *when he can free-associate*."[2] Creating an environment in which a person can discover this inherent capacity seems to me to be healing in its own right. As the British child psychotherapist Adam Phillips has written, "It is only when two people forget themselves, in each other's presence, that they can recognize each other."[3] Psychotherapy, like meditation, hinges on showing us a new way to be with ourselves, and with others. Whether we learn this from meditation or therapy is not the important thing. What matters is that we learn it at all.

I have divided this book into four parts, based on the nicknames that Tibetan Buddhists sometimes give to their spiritual practices. In the Tibetan tradition, the closest available comparison to the joy of meditation is the experience of simultaneously forgetting and discovering oneself that occurs in falling in love. Thus, the four levels of practice are often referred to as Looking, Smiling, Embracing, and Orgasm. There is a common happiness in each of these states—the joy of momentarily dropping the ego boundaries that prevent us from connecting with one another.

I have taken these four states and used them to present the essence of what I have learned from meditation and psychotherapy over the past twenty-five years. In organizing the book in this way, I have woven together the accumulated wisdom of

Buddhism and psychotherapy to show how the happiness that we seek depends on our ability to balance the ego's need to *do* with our inherent capacity to *be*. I have mixed the teachings of various schools of Buddhism with those of therapy to show how the two grand traditions can work together to enhance one another. Implicit and explicit throughout the text is the understanding that meditative wisdom does not have to be isolated from daily life. Our need to expand awareness beyond our isolated egos is as necessary in relationships as it is in meditation.

When the Zen master kept pouring tea into the professor's cup, he was trying to shock him into a new way of seeing himself. He wanted him to tune into the empty space of his mind rather than identify only with its contents. In the same way I hope that the material in this book can provoke in the reader a new experience of the self. As my roommate Steve's experience taught me, there is a difference between accumulating knowledge and discovering wisdom. As my Buddhist teachers have shown me, wisdom emerges in the space around words as much as from language itself.

part one

LOOKING

starting where you are

Emptiness has been said by the Conquerors (Buddhas) to be the relinquishment of views, but they have said that those who hold to the view of emptiness are incurable.

NAGARJUNA

1

e m p t i n e s s

Emboldened by the discovery, in my sixteenth year, of Samuel Beckett's bleak view of the human landscape, I took an informal poll of all forty-seven members of my high school class and asked who among them was bothered by an inner sense of emptiness or insufficiency. Only the captain of the football team, a good-natured but decidedly unintellectual fellow, did not admit to harboring such a feeling. I felt empowered by my discovery. Excited even. Perhaps this troubling image of myself as *not quite right* was more universal than I had thought.

For years I had been haunted by this feeling. Sometimes I thought of it as an emptiness in my chest, sometimes as an impossible longing in my heart, and sometimes as a sense that other people were more real than I was. I had a recurring dream during that time of suddenly discovering, through a variety of means, a secret room in my house that was my one special place. I can still picture, or rather, feel, that room today. It was hidden behind a fake wall and was reached through a secret corridor or back staircase. Every time I came upon it in my dreams I felt relieved. It had the odd combination of seeming totally strange (the light was different, the furniture was different, even the air was different) and yet completely comfortable. In the rest of my life, however, with the notable exception of certain private moments in my nascent intimate life, this sense of comfort was absent.

I carried this feeling of insufficiency with me when I went off to college, but it was not until my sophomore year at Harvard that I went to the University Health Services and asked to see a therapist. I assured myself that things were really okay and that this foray into therapy would be an interesting diversion. In my heart I knew that I was still troubled by the emptiness I had approached in high school. I was searching for that secret room of my dreams. I had begun to take psychology courses, had read more of the popular literature of the times, and, encouraged by the results of my high school poll, I was now more open with my friends about such feelings. I figured there must be someone, provided by the university, who could help me understand them better. I was looking for a way to deal with my emptiness once and for all.

The therapist who was assigned to me was an impeccably dressed and elegantly appointed psychiatrist who was a practitioner, I later discovered, of short-term psychodynamic psychotherapy. He was a tall, fit man with a long, handsome face, long fingers folded carefully over his knees, and huge feet with polished leather shoes that shone like a bathroom sink. I had never seen such fabulous suits as he wore. I remember him nodding gravely as I described what I was feeling and as I gave him the requested details of my family upbringing. He seemed to take my emptiness very seriously. By the end of my second session he told me that I did not need to come back anymore. My problem was very simple, he said. It had to do with the pressure I was feeling to make certain career choices, which was a sign of my "Oedipus complex." If I could just understand that, he explained, I would start to feel better.

I had taken a number of psychology courses by this time but had found Freud unreadable and could make no sense of this interpretation. I knew that the Oedipus complex had something to do with my father and that he was implying that my emptiness stemmed from a feeling of competition with him, but this explanation rolled off of me like a bead of sweat before I was out the door. I left reassured that my condition had a name but otherwise untouched by my encounter. I had come looking for an experience but left with only an explanation.

A year or so later, when meeting my first meditation instructors, I learned to interpret my emptiness in a completely different way. "Stop trying to understand what you are feeling and just feel," they told me. "Absence or presence, it doesn't matter. Just pay attention to everything exactly as it appears and *don't judge it.*" They taught me to use awareness of my breathing as a model for attention to difficult emotional states. "Don't try to control the breath," they counselled. "Breathing happens on its own. Let the breath breathe *you.* Pay attention to whatever sensation, or lack of sensation, you can find."

In meditation, I had stumbled upon a new way to be with myself. I did not have to make that disturbing feeling of emptiness disappear. I did not have to run away from my emptiness, or cure it, or eradicate it. I had only to see what was actually there. In fact, far from being "empty," I found that emptiness was a rather "full" feeling. I discovered that emptiness was the canvas, or background, of my being. I did not understand it, but I was much less afraid. My condition had no name, but I could reach down into it.

the mustard seed

There is a well-known story in the Buddhist tradition, the story of Kisagotami and the mustard seed, that illustrates how Buddhism uses the experience of emptiness to cultivate spiritual maturity.[1] Like most good Buddhist stories, it can be understood on several levels. A young woman named

Kisagotami lost her only child to illness around the time of his first birthday. Bereft, she went from house to house in her village, clasping the dead child to her breast and pleading for medicine to revive him. Her neighbors, thinking her mad, were frightened and did their best to avoid her entreaties. However, one man sought to help her by directing her to the Buddha, telling her that he had the medicine she was seeking. Kisagotami went to the Buddha, as we go to our psychotherapists, and begged him for the medicine.

"I know of some," he promised, "but I will need a handful of mustard seed from a house where no child, husband, parent, or servant has died."

Making her rounds in the village, Kisagotami slowly came to realize that such a house was not to be found. Putting the body of her child down in the forest, she made her way back to where the Buddha was camped.

"Have you procured the handful of mustard seed?" he asked.

"I have not," she replied. "The people of the village told me, 'The living are few, but the dead are many.' "

"You thought that you alone had lost a son," said the Buddha. "The law of death is that among all living creatures there is no permanence."

Some time later, when Kisagotami had become a renunciate and follower of the Buddha, she was standing on a hillside engaged in a task when she looked out toward the village in the distance and saw the lights in the houses shining.

"My state is like those lamps," she reflected, and the Buddha is said to have sent her a vision of himself at that moment confirming her vision.

"All living beings resemble the flame of these lamps," he told her, "one moment lighted, the next extinguished; those only who have arrived at Nirvana are at rest."[2]

While this story is first and foremost a parable about death and impermanence, it also is a vivid story about the questions of emptiness. Clutching her dead baby to her breast the way we hold on to our feelings of emotional deprivation, Kisagotami searched for a way to bring her emptiness back to life. Demanding of her fellow villagers the way we demand of our families and therapists that the problem be *taken care of,* she came to see that her individual problem was not unique, that it was universal. Redirecting her gaze from her own trauma to the flickering lights of the village, she achieved a breakthrough: She saw the more universal experience that her own particular misfortune obscured. It was only by facing, not denying, her personal tragedy that Kisagotami could uncover this greater reality. By struggling with and accepting her loss, she could understand the Buddha's teachings. No longer striving to contain her grief and keep herself together, she nevertheless stopped falling apart. By appreciating that she could never have what she thought she deserved, she was able to relax. Her emptiness stopped overtaking her only when she stopped taking it personally.

sparks of emptiness

By the time I began my clinical training as a psychiatrist, I had dug down further into my own feelings of emptiness through a combination of intensive meditation and further psychotherapy. I arrived at the psychiatric hospital where I was to work for the next four years not particularly surprised to find that the great bulk of my patients also suffered from some version of these now familiar feelings. I was unsure at first how to translate the Buddha's insights into actual clinical practice and yielded to the generally prevailing climate at the hospital as I began my work as a therapist. It was the early eighties, and there was a kind of revolt going on against the caricature of the dour, silent psychotherapist. People need mirroring, the theory went, in order to become secure in their own reality, and so I tried, in accordance with this idea, to reflect back some warmth to my patients.

The model for this approach to therapy came from observations of infants and parents. When a child does a new task, it was noted, she will turn back quickly to check if her mother is watching. Catching the twinkle in her mother's eye, she will be empowered to keep going, and she will take her mother's approval, or affirmation, with her into the new activity. Self-esteem and self-assurance grow in proportion to how mirrored a child feels. When this process is inadequate, the child feels empty. The empty self needs a real relationship with a real person in order to discover its own reality.

This orientation did much to humanize the kind of teaching I received: It gave a theoretical justification to what many were already feeling and allowed skilled therapists to break down the self-conscious edifice that had alienated many a struggling patient. But this approach, while appealing, seemed sometimes to have serious flaws when put into practice. In my own early work as a therapist I hoped vigorously that my own "unconditional positive regard" would help my patients consolidate their selves and relieve their suffering. More often than not, however, I found that, from their point of view, I could not do enough. They wanted more and more of me, and I would find myself embroiled in their lives. Phone calls came between sessions, demands for attention escalated, and I began to feel exhausted and depleted, more like a beleaguered parent than a mirroring, supportive one.

In my final year of training as a psychiatrist, I found myself in the unenviable position of having the chief psychiatrist of the hospital, a psychoanalyst named Otto Kernberg, as my primary ongoing supervisor. Before entering the program, a sympathetic friend in the psychiatric community had taken me aside and warned me to keep my interests in meditation quiet while working for Kernberg.

"If he hears about it, he'll eat you alive," he warned me.

Austrian by birth but raised in Chile, Dr. Kernberg was the leading expert in the problem of emptiness in the psychoanalytic world. Kernberg taught that emptiness was the result of defects in self-development that interfered with a child's ability to integrate the idea of one person having both good and bad qualities. In Kernberg's view, the infant first keeps "all-good" and "all-bad" experiences separate; she has no idea that the mother who gratifies her hunger is the same person as the mother who is not there immediately when she cries. At some point, if the child's frustration and anger are handled properly, she will have the realization that the gratifying and frustrating mother are one and the same person and will thus have the ability to relate to "real" people, not just to what he called "part-objects." Feelings of emptiness, thought Kernberg, occurred when this ability to relate to "whole-objects" was lacking. Often masking a virulent rage or self-hatred, emptiness, for Kernberg, was a sign of lack of cohesiveness in the self, of an inability to tolerate conflicting feelings for the same person.

Dr. Kernberg (or "Otto," as we all called him behind his back) was much feared in my milieu, having cultivated a rather aggressive and unforgiving persona to go along with his theory (or vice versa), but much to my relief, I found him generous, patient, and quite forthcoming in a personal way, more relaxed within the privacy of his own office than I would have expected. Yet on one point he was very focused. My problems with my demanding patients lay, he felt, in my failure to deal with their aggression. Unable to see me as a real, and therefore limited, person, they were expecting me to be "all-good," and at the same time, they were completely furious with me.

"Tell them you don't think they are aware of how much they want to destroy you," he would say. "Show them this pattern in their lives, how they ruin that which they most need."

Indeed, these interpretations were extremely helpful when I put them into my own words and found ways of communicating their essence to my patients. They were able to settle down and make real progress in their lives. Their disturbing complaints of unreality and depersonalization went away. But even as these same patients matured psychologically, their core feeling of emptiness did not disappear. I began to wonder to myself what was wrong. What was I learning from my meditation teachers that I was not communicating to my patients?

At about this time, I was invited to a small colloquium of therapists and meditation instructors designed to stimulate discussion of links between psychotherapy and Buddhism. Preoccupied with my patients' problem, I asked one of the Tibetan lamas if he could clarify the relationship between my kind of emptiness (and that which I was trying to treat in my patients) and the emptiness that is extolled in Buddhist teachings. I had come to the conclusion myself that the two emptinesses could not have much in common except the sharing of a name. And yet I knew from my own experience that there was a connection between the two, one that I did not yet completely understand.

I knew that emptiness (or *sunyata*), from a Buddhist perspective, was an understanding of one's true nature, an intuition of the absence of inherent identity in people or in things. It was the core psychological truth of Buddhism. Emptiness, from a Western perspective, seemed to me to be a tortured feeling of distress, an absence of vitality, a sense of being not quite real enough, of disconnection. I put my question to Gelek Rinpoche ("Rinpoche" being an honorific title like "doctor" or "professor"), a Cambridge-educated lama who now teaches at the University of Michigan, but I was fairly confident of my own formulation and was not quite paying full attention as he began to reply.

With an uncharacteristically serious expression, the lama was making what looked like a hammering motion with his hands over and over again, as if waiting for me to tune in to what he was saying. "It is like a blacksmith," he was saying, "striking on a . . . what do you call it in English? . . . striking on an anvil." I could not follow what he was getting at; I had trouble even understanding his words. "These are like sparks of emptiness," he went on, making upward motions with his fingers to show the sparks flying off of the anvil. "These are minds striking against emptiness, like a blacksmith strikes against his anvil. The hollowness you describe, the deficiency and distress, these are like sparks of emptiness, untrained minds trying to grasp emptiness."

The implications of Gelek's statement for the psychotherapy profession leaped out at me. "Stop trying to eliminate emptiness!" he was saying. This is where Western therapy was going wrong. Like their patients, psychotherapists were intimidated by emptiness. They were struggling to take those feelings of insufficiency that I had struggled with since high school and eradicate them. They tried to "get to the roots" of the problem, to solve the puzzle, to uncover the hidden dynamics and come up with a plausible *explanation,* much as my first therapist had handed me my Oedipus complex and expected it to cure me. Therapists were trying to get rid of emptiness by uncovering its cause. From Freud and his followers on down, therapists had identified all kinds of plausible causes.

Psychotherapy was holding out for a cure. Buddhism, as I was learning, sought to turn the Western experience of emptiness around. "Don't be so afraid of it," Gelek was saying. "You can never understand what the Buddhists mean if you are so afraid of your personal emptiness." The problem with the Western experience of emptiness was that it was mixed with so much fear.

I thought at once of a disturbing trend I had witnessed at the psychiatric hospital where I worked. The patients, many of whom were struggling with intense versions of just these feelings, were kept at arms' length by the staff, disparaged as "borderline," and talked about as if they needed a "cure," while the staff, in their sometimes internecine dealings with each other and in their private supervisions, were every bit as borderline as the patients they were looking down on. They were as confused about themselves as the patients were, and they acted out in similar, if not quite so blatant, ways. They alternately idealized and devalued their authority figures, crossed ego boundaries with their patients and with each other, and were just as sensitive to abandonment and criticism as were the people in their care.

In our zeal to eliminate the ghosts of our childhood, to nourish the empty places of emotional insufficiency, and to achieve that pinnacle of psychological development that the British psychoanalyst D. W. Winnicott called "feeling real," we were treating feelings of emptiness as something that needed to be fixed and cured and therefore losing the ground upon which we rest. Our aversion to emptiness is such that we have become expert at explaining it away, distancing ourselves from it, or assigning blame for its existence on the past or on the faults of others. We contaminate it with our personal histories and expect that it will disappear when we have resolved our personal problems. Thus, Western psychotherapists are trained to understand a report of emptiness as indicative of a deficiency in someone's emotional upbringing, a defect in character, a defense against overwhelming feelings of aggression, or as a stand-in for feelings of inadequacy. Since most of us share one or more of these traits, it becomes all too easy to pathologize a feeling that in Buddhism serves as a starting place for self-exploration.

As Gelek Rinpoche indicated, emptiness can never be eliminated, although the experience of it can be transformed. Like sparks flying off of the blacksmith's anvil, experiences of emptiness are part of the fabric of our being. Emptiness appears first as the dark side of our attempts to create a separate and self-sufficient self. Any therapy that tries to explain it away, or cure it with a corrective emotional experience, is destined to produce frustration and disappointment. Only when we stop fighting with our personal emptiness can we begin to appreciate the transformation that is possible. The most psychological of the world's religions, and the most spiritual of the world's psychologies, Buddhism authenticates a feeling that nearly all Westerners seek to deny, that psychotherapy endeavors, unsuccessfully, to eradicate.

the capacity to be alone

As I reflected on my encounter with Gelek, I pondered my own experiences of meditation. I knew I felt better when I stopped distancing myself from my own emptiness. Meditation had taught me how to separate out the fear of emptiness from my experience of it. Emptiness did not have to mean annihilation, I had realized, nor did it have to mean nothingness. By looking into my own emptiness, I had paradoxically discovered more of my own voice. If therapy could target the *fear* of emptiness instead of trying to wipe out the entire feeling, perhaps it would be more effective. What *was* this feeling, really, but the sense that I did not know who I was? Why should that be so objectionable? What I had learned from Buddhism was that I did not have to know myself analytically as much as I had to tolerate not knowing.

This line of reasoning led me directly to a potent undercurrent in the writings of psychoanalyst D. W. Winnicott. Winnicott taught that to go willingly into unknowing was the key to living a full life. Only if a parent provides what he called "good-enough ego coverage" can a child go without fear into the unknown. As he explained it, a child needs to develop the capacity to be alone: a faith or trust in the relationship with the parent such that it is possible to explore the world outside of it.

From the beginning, suggested Winnicott, the mother's task is greater than just satisfying her baby's physical needs, greater even than mirroring. She must also be able to leave her child alone. This leaving alone does not mean ignoring, nor does it necessarily mean physically, or literally, looking away. An infant, after all, has to be attended to almost constantly. Leaving alone means allowing a child to have her own experience, whether alone or when feeding, bathing, or being held. When suspended in the matrix of the parent-child relationship, a child is free to explore, to venture into new territory, both within herself and without. This freedom to explore while held within the safety net of the parent's benign presence develops into the capacity to be alone.

I was reminded of this when on vacation in Maine with my family recently. I came upstairs one evening to find my seven-year-old son alone in his darkening room with his nose pressed against the screen of the open window in his bedroom. "The air smells so sweet here," he said dreamily. Alone in his room, he was having a new, and unexpected, experience. His senses were expanding his reality.

Of all the therapists whom I had read or studied with, Winnicott seemed to me the most attuned to the issue of emptiness. With too much interference from the parents, or too much absence, a child is forced to spend her mental energy coping with her parents' intrusiveness or unavailability instead of exploring herself. This mental energy then takes over, leading to a situation in which the child's thinking mind becomes the locus of her existence and the child feels empty. If my son had been worried over where I was, or how I was doing, he could not have smelled the air. When the relationship with a parent is too fragile, a child naturally tries to compensate. This leads to the development of a precocious "caretaker self" that is tinged with a feeling of falsity. Besides feeling empty, a person in this predicament also fears emptiness. The fear of emptiness is really a sign of the fragility of the bond with the parent. We are afraid to venture into the unknown because to do so would remind us of how unsafe we once felt. This fear, taught Winnicott, is of being "infinitely dropped," or, perhaps, of being infinitely reminded.

What connected me even more assuredly to Winnicott's explanation of emptiness was his insistence that overcoming the fear of emptiness requires "a new experience in a specialized setting."[3] This was precisely what I had found in meditation. Without the counselling of my meditation teachers, and without the method of nonjudgmental awareness, I could never have done the unimaginable thing of looking into my own emptiness. I could not have tolerated that degree of aloneness nor would I have been willing to drop my compensatory mind. Meditation gave me the faith that there were other techniques of self-exploration than the analysis of my thinking mind. It gave me a way of getting back to the secret room of my dreams. I became convinced that therapy could function for people in a similar manner.

The Buddhist way of working with the mind has profound implications for how we as individuals think about change. In Western theories, the hope is always that emptiness can be healed, that if the character is developed or the trauma resolved that the background feelings will diminish. If we can make the ego stronger, the expectation is that emptiness will go away. In Buddhism, the approach is reversed. Focus on the emptiness, the dissatisfaction, and the feelings of imperfection, and the character will get stronger. Learn how to tolerate nothing and your mind will be at rest. Psychotherapy tends to focus on the personal melodrama, exploring its origins and trying to clean up its mess. Buddhism seeks, instead, to purify the insight of emptiness.

Emptiness is vast and astonishing, the Buddhist approach insists; it does not have to be toxic. When we grasp the emptiness of our false selves, we are touching a little bit of truth. If we can relax into that truth, we can discover ourselves in a new way. But without a method of looking into emptiness, most of us are at risk of becoming overwhelmed by fear. In meditation, there is such a method for looking into emptiness without being overtaken by the fear of the disconnections of the past.

This is a lesson that I have had to apply again and again in my work as a therapist because this fear is precisely what troubles many of the people who come to me for help. People are afraid to face the old sadnesses that lurk in their bodies and psyches and that date from failures in their past. They are afraid to face them, but they are plagued by a sense of falseness if they do not, and so they feel stuck. They actually come to therapy not just because they are afraid, but because somewhere within themselves they are searching for a way to go more deeply into those painful places. It is part of our drive for wholeness that we need to connect up with the agonies of the past. The emphasis in Buddhism on acceptance and meditation rather than talking and analyzing is something that Western therapy can learn from.

Meditation has taught me that people can tolerate more than they think. I often find myself in the position of a coach, teaching people how to venture into their own unexperienced feelings. Psychotherapy, while conventionally seeking to eradicate the debilitating sense of emptiness, can also serve as a forum for authenticating and encouraging a capacity to bear the unknowability of the self. When a patient says to me, as a frustrated and anxious young woman named Betsy did the other day, "I just want to be somewhere where *I'm* not," I do not automatically rush to judgment.

"I know what you mean," I answered. "Let's talk about how you could actually have that experience." I explained to Betsy that there were healthy ways as well as unhealthy ways of dropping the oppressive feeling of the self. While people tend to turn first to the unhealthy ways, such as using drugs or alcohol, there are actually much more fulfilling ways of losing oneself, of which meditation is a good example.

At the same time as Betsy was trying to get away from hated aspects of herself, or internalized remnants of her intrusive mother, or (more to the point) the pain and pressure of her own anger, she was also reaching for a new experience. She needed to know that her urge was not merely pathological. As she began to explore around the edge of her recurrent worries, she discovered an anxiety in her chest that seemed to run through her like a hollow core.

At first she was deeply afraid of that place. With some encouragement, though, Betsy learned to rest her attention in the hollow core, and she saw that it was a rich source of mysterious feeling, sometimes sad and lonely but at other times filled with the energy and inquisitiveness of a young child. The hollow space became an enriching space as well as a scary one, filled with unanticipated qualities that expanded her sense of her own reality.

Like my son smelling the night air, Betsy began to use her senses to break through her self-limiting conceptions. She was not just a "bad" girl who could not "make nice" with her mother, she was a passionate young woman whose love and imagination had been stifled by her difficulties getting along in her family. Although Betsy had fought with her mother to preserve herself from her mother's criticisms, she emerged from those long years with an identity that was forged completely in reaction to her mother. Needless to say, this was very limiting. Only by going into the hollow core could Betsy retrieve the rest of herself.[4]

In a similar vein, after breaking up his ten-year marriage a good friend of mine, complaining of intolerable emptiness, sought psychotherapy at a local mental health clinic. His only wish, he told his new therapist in their first meeting, was to be free from what he was feeling, and he implored his therapist to take his pain away. His therapist, however, had just left a Zen community where she had been in residence for three years. She was assigned to be my friend's therapist completely by chance since he was by no means seeking a therapist with a meditative orientation. When he approached her with his complaints, she urged him to stay with his feelings, no matter how intolerable they seemed. She did not attempt to reassure him nor to help him change what he was feeling, but complimented him on being in touch with such an essential truth. When he would complain of his anxiety or his loneliness, she would encourage him to feel them more intensely, and she confronted him repeatedly when he tried to flee from her injunctions. While my friend did not feel any better, he was intrigued by his therapist's approach, and he began to practice a beginning form of daily meditation that he learned outside of the therapeutic setting.

He describes one pivotal moment in his meditation as a turning point. Terribly uncomfortable with the itchings, burnings, pressures, and pains of his practice and unable to simply stay with the sensations, he remembers finally watching the entire crescendo of an itch. Seeing it develop, crest, and disappear while not making any move to scratch it, he suddenly realized what his therapist had meant when she counselled him to stay with his emotional state, and from that moment on his depression began to lift. Rather than trying to strengthen his ego by eliminating his emptiness, my friend's therapist had done the reverse. By encouraging his capacity to stay with emptiness, she helped his ego become stronger. His feelings began to change only when he dropped the desire to change them.[5]

My meditation teacher, Joseph Goldstein, tells a story about one of his most profound spiritual experiences that, to my mind, illustrates a similar point about the value of learning to bear emptiness. Joseph was doing a retreat, called a *sesshin,* with a very powerful Zen teacher named Sasaki Roshi and was working with a form of meditation known as koan practice, in which he was forced to struggle with a problem, or riddle, that has no rational answer. The *sesshin* is structured very tightly and Joseph saw the roshi, or teacher, four times a day to give him his koan answers. But each time he answered, the roshi would ring his bell very quickly and dismiss him, saying things like, "Oh, very stupid," or "Okay, but not Zen," leading Joseph to feel more and more frustrated, demeaned, and tense. Finally the roshi seemed to relent a bit, and he gave Joseph a new, simpler koan, "How do you manifest the Buddha while chanting a sutra?" Joseph understood that the point was to come in and just chant a bit, rather than to try to give some kind of rational explanation, but there was one problem that made the exercise much more complicated.

As Joseph describes it, "I do not think Sasaki Roshi knew, although he might have known, that this koan plugged in exactly to some very deep conditioning in me going back to the third grade. Our singing teacher back then had said, 'Goldstein, just mouth the words.' From then on I have had a tremendous inhibition about singing, and now here I was, having to perform in a very charged situation. I was a total wreck. In the pressure cooker of the *sesshin*, which is held in silence except for the interviews, everything becomes magnified so much.

"I rehearsed and rehearsed two lines of chant, all the while getting more and more tight, more and more tense. The bell rang for the interview, I went in, I started chanting, and I messed up the entire thing. I got all the words wrong; I felt completely exposed and vulnerable and raw. And Roshi just looked at me and with great feeling said, 'Very good.' "[6]

Joseph had been hiding this particular inadequacy, and yet, as the intensity of his feelings revealed, he had remained much identified with it. Sasaki Roshi helped him open up to the very vulnerability that Joseph was struggling to avoid. He helped him to *be*: open and vulnerable and insecure, not confident, controlled, and coherent. By making Joseph's own childhood emptiness accessible to him once again, and by focusing on it, Roshi unleashed the power of Joseph's mature mind to be empty. Relieved of the associated shame and humiliation, he no longer feared, in Huang Po's words, an infinite drop through the Void. Uncontaminated, his own own personal emptiness became his ticket to ride.

Joseph's story reminds me of an experience I had hearing Tibetan monks from the Namgyal Monastery doing their ritual harmonic chanting. When listening to the monks, at first all I could hear were their low gutteral rumblings, just as all that I hear at first in meditation are my own obsessive worries and fears. But then, off in the distance, comes a sweet, eerie, high note rising above the fray, hovering there, its existence dependent on the simultaneous appearance of the rumbling lower octaves. The monks are actually producing a new note, an overtone, that is one of the most beautiful sounds I have ever heard. In the same way in meditation, I have experienced clearings in my mind just when I seemed the most stuck.[7]

Our personal feelings of emptiness are like the low, gutteral rumblings of the Tibetan monks chanting. At first they are all we can hear. But then, slowly, or sometimes suddenly, something sweet emerges out of the depths of our own minds. Gradually, the overtone fills our consciousness and we cannot believe what we are hearing. Our own personal and self-centered emptiness yields to something more universal. The sparks of emptiness return to their source.

This is the task that faces nearly all of us. We must learn how to be with our feelings of emptiness without rushing to change them. Only then can we have access to the still, silent center of our own awareness that has been hiding, unbeknownst to our caretaker selves, behind our own embarrassment and shame. When we tap in to this secret storehouse, we begin to appreciate the two-faced nature of emptiness—it fills us with dissatisfaction as it opens us to our own mystery. As the Buddhist traditions always insist, if we look outside of ourselves for relief from our own predicament, we are sure to come up short. Only by learning how to touch the ground of our own emptiness can we feel whole again.

2

surrender

When I was first learning about Buddhist meditation
I remember becoming inescapably aware of how much tension
I was carrying in my shoulders. I had not yet turned twenty-
one and had gone to Boulder, Colorado, for a kind of spiritual
summer camp organized by a young Tibetan Buddhist lama,
Chögyam Trungpa, Rinpoche. Trungpa had fled his native
country, been educated in England, and attracted a number of
followers in the United States. A graduate student friend of
mine had told me about the summer program, and I was im-
pressed with how many of my cultural heroes were teaching
there: John Cage, Gregory Bateson, Ram Dass, and Allen
Ginsberg were among the faculty, as were American Buddhist

teachers Jack Kornfield, Joseph Goldstein, and Sharon Salzberg.

There were thousands of people in attendance that first summer of the Naropa Institute. At one point I was sitting on a hill overlooking a parking lot in downtown Boulder, and I saw beneath me an old Volkswagen bus with a huge Sanskrit *om* painted on its roof, winding its way into town. I thought I was seeing the future: the coming together of East and West.

While there were scores of eminent and accomplished teachers in Boulder that summer, many of whose offerings I eagerly sampled, my first real teachers were a pair of twins from Long Island who had been randomly assigned to be my roommates. Sons of Jewish immigrants who had set up a family fruit and vegetable business, these twins had become experts in such esoteric knowledge as herbal medicine, diet, naturopathy, massage, and Chinese philosophy. Eschewing most of the formal courses at Naropa, with a not so carefully disguised disdain for the egos of most of the faculty, they contented themselves with regular early morning drives to Denver's wholesale fruit and vegetable market.

I was taking classes in Buddhist meditation, Chinese tai chi, sensory awareness, and contact improvisation dance while they were accumulating boxes of ripe figs, peaches, nectarines, and cherries. They watched me with amusement as I took course after course, fruitlessly struggling to release the shoulder tension that I could no longer ignore. Finally, one of the twins offered to teach me to juggle.

My breakthrough that summer came not during any formal meditation practice but from my experience of juggling. As I finally became able to keep three balls in the air, I noticed suddenly how quiet my mind had become. My everyday thoughts had vanished, and the tension in my shoulders was gone. I was momentarily undefended and curiously at peace. I wasn't trying to relax, and I wasn't trying not to relax. Everything was floating. I was no longer centered in my thinking mind.

being nobody

I remember this experience when I try to bring what I have learned from meditation to my practice of psychotherapy. People come to me most often because they are unhappy with how cut off they feel, not because they are not separate or individuated enough. The traditional view of therapy as building up the ego simply does not do justice to what people's needs actually are. Most of us have developed our egos enough; what we suffer from is the accumulated tension of that development. We have trouble surrendering ourselves as I was momentarily able to do while juggling. I have searched for a long time to find an acceptable psychoanalytic explanation for the healing effects of this loss of ego.

In Buddhism, of course, the cultivation of such states is key. But in psychoanalysis, while there is a long tradition of fascination with mystical states, there is an equally long tradition of reducing those states to their infantile derivatives. Most commonly in psychoanalysis, the early preverbal and preconceptual mind of the infant is idealized into a blissful state of union with the mother in which the newborn is thought to dwell. This early state of oneness is treated as a kind of Garden of Eden by the psychoanalysts, who then interpret any spiritual urge as seeking, in Freud's words, "a restoration of limitless narcissism" and the "resurrection of infantile helplessness."[1] Was my breakthrough in juggling merely the equivalent of a good feed?

More sympathetic psychoanalysts, attempting to carve out a place for spiritual experience, adapted the orthodox view a tiny bit. These experiences are not purely regressive, they argue, they are also valuable. In evoking the outgrown mother-child bond, they function as a kind of protective talisman against fears of separateness and isolation. The psychoanalyst Ernst Kris coined the phrase "regression in service of the ego" to explain this view.

According to his argument, spiritual experiences have the potential to open a window into the past, to enable one to reexamine and reexperience unresolved conflicts while working with them in a new arena. In this view, my mastery of juggling might have helped me gain confidence in my ability to take care of myself, an ability that I had not properly inte-

32

grated in my childhood. The "adaptive" nature of my regression could be differentiated from a more "pathological" regression by virtue of its transitory, reversible nature and its ability to increase my self-esteem.[2]

Most of the more humanistic psychologists who had found their way to Naropa that summer would, of course, have nothing to do with such old-fashioned formulations. My discovery was a transcendent one, they would argue, taking me to a level "beyond" the ego, to a stage of development more evolved than the everyday mind. Perhaps I had had what the psychologist Abraham Maslow had called a "peak experience," or maybe I had peeked in at a state of consciousness more evolved than our ordinary "suboptimal" one. On the path of personal growth, perhaps I was progressing from a hierarchy of basic ego needs to a higher level where spiritual concerns predominate.

The transcendent should not be confused with the regressive, argued the writer Ken Wilber, the premier theoretician of the New Age. Wilber described what he called the "pre/trans fallacy," the tendency of both psychologists and spiritual practitioners to mix up and confuse infantile (pre-egoic) and transcendent (post-egoic) levels of development. Assuming that mystical states are nothing but regressions is as wrong as assuming that early childhood experiences can never be reconfigured in spiritual states, wrote Wilber. The pre/trans fallacy is a "mixture of pre-egoic fantasy with trans-egoic vision, of pre-

conceptual feelings with transconceptual insight, of preper-
sonal desires with transpersonal growth, of pre-egoic whoopee
with trans-egoic liberation. . . ."[3]

Wilber's contributions seemed to satisfy many people because he answered the sometimes vexing question of what we
need the ego for. "You have to be *some*body before you can be
*no*body," people began to say. Life is a journey, a path, a series
of stages or steps or levels of development. The ego must be
formed before it can be dismantled; the self must be consoli-
dated before it can be transcended. Perhaps my breakthrough
signalled the threshold of a new level of consciousness, the first
strike against the ego.

While Wilber's insights were appealing to me, I nevertheless harbored doubts about them. My study of Buddhism did
not support a linear line of development. Meditation was
about bringing awareness to everyday life, not about escaping
it. The self was *never* real, taught the Buddha. The task of
meditation is to discover what has always been true about the
nature of self, its fundamental unreality. In the words of the
Dalai Lama that came to haunt me, "This seemingly solid,
concrete, independent, self-instituting 'I' under its own power
that appears actually does not exist at all."[4] The sense of self
only *seems* solid, he says. It "appears" to us as "concrete, independent," self-created, and "under its own power," but this is,
in fact, an illusion.

The true nature of self is something else entirely. Meditation is meant to open a window into this something else; it is not meant to eradicate a previously existent ego. Somebody and nobody are interdependent: They feed off of each other rather than succeeding one another.

There is a well-known poem by Wallace Stevens, "Thirteen Ways of Looking at a Blackbird," that a patient of mine quoted to me one day, which gives a sense of what the Dalai Lama means by the nonexistence of the self that appears. The poem contains the following verse:

> I do not know which to prefer,
> The beauty of inflections
> Or the beauty of innuendoes,
> The blackbird whistling
> Or just after.[5]

When we speak of the self from the perspective of Western psychology, we are most often taken with the beauty of inflection, with the self's whistle as it appears. But when we look at the self from the perspective of the Buddhist psychologies, we emphasize the beauty of the self's innuendo, of the space around the self.

So perhaps my juggling breakthrough was the equivalent of hearing the blackbird's whistle "just after." I did not need to leave my ego behind, merely to see around its edges. My shoulder tension and my reliance on my thinking mind were symptoms of a defensive reliance on only one aspect of my nature: a holding on to the self "as it appears." While I was juggling, as sometimes happens in meditation, my perspective had been broadened. I had permitted a loosening that was neither transcendent nor regressive but that had allowed me to see in three dimensions instead of in two. I had glimpsed my ego's inherent unreality, or rather, I had permitted myself to simply be, without worrying about keeping myself together.

relaxing the self

"In thinking of the psychology of mysticism," D. W. Winnicott wrote, "it is usual to concentrate on the understanding of the mystic's withdrawal into a personal inner world. . . . Perhaps not enough attention has been paid to the mystic's retreat to a position in which he can communicate secretly with subjective . . . phenomena, the loss of contact with the world of shared reality being counterbalanced by a gain in terms of feeling real."[6]

When Winnicott wrote of communicating secretly with subjective phenomena, he was alluding to a mode of being that he described over and over again in his work. Contrasting such a state to one of either ego *integration* or *disintegration*, Winnicott wrote instead of the experiences of *unintegration* or letting go. By *unintegrated* Winnicott meant something like what I had stumbled upon in my juggling where the usual need for control is suspended and where the self can unwind. He meant losing oneself without feeling lost, hearing the self's innuendo rather than just its inflection. "The opposite of integration would seem to be disintegration," commented Winnicott. "That is only partly true. The opposite, initially, requires a word like unintegration. Relaxation for an infant means not feeling a need to integrate, the mother's ego-supportive function being taken for granted."[7]

It is the mother's function, in Winnicott's view, to create an environment for her baby in which it is safe to be nobody, because it is only out of such a place that the infant can begin to find herself. "It is not so much a question of giving the baby satisfaction," he wrote, "as of letting the baby find and come to terms with the object (breast, bottle, milk, etc.)."[8] As in the Wallace Stevens poem about the blackbird, the mother must do more than just satisfy the baby's basic needs; she must also create a space in which the infant can discover herself.

The mother is responsible for background as well as foreground, Winnicott implied. She must let the baby find the object, not just provide it immediately. When this space is offered to a child, it develops into the capacity for unrestricted, unimpaired awareness that becomes the foundation for looking *in* to the self in later years. By accessing this ability we are able to *feel* our way into our selves just as the infant learns to explore her early environment.

A friend of mine made his own version of this discovery

once when he spoke to me of his difficulties in relating to his ten-month-old daughter. He had trouble, he said, finding "the right voice" to talk to her in. He could talk baby talk, read to her, play games, and give her direction, but he worried that he sounded fake, like his own mother, when he talked to her. I suggested that he try being silent with her, that he was worrying too much about *how* he talked to her. There are other types of communication besides verbal, I reminded him.

A parent needs to discover how to *hold* a child not just physically but in silence. In fostering a state of unintegration by being present but not interfering, a parent creates a holding environment that nourishes a child. In so doing she sustains and encourages her child's psychic life, in a way that my friend instinctively knew that he was not doing. When my friend experienced a sense of falseness with his daughter, he was aware of the artificial nature of his interaction. On some level, he knew that he was not giving her the chance to relax. She had to remain on guard, mobilized to respond to her father's anxiety. She could not float away into her own experience. My friend was setting up a situation in which his daughter would have to stay too attentive to him and too afraid of the depths of her own self.

The capacity to be alone is a paradox since it can only be developed with someone else in the room. Once it is developed, the child trusts that she will not be intruded upon and permits herself a secret communication with private and personal phenomena. The best adult model that Winnicott could find for this is what he called "after intercourse," when each person is content to be alone but is not withdrawn.[9] This is a very unusual state because of how little anxiety exists. There are no questions about the other person's availability, but there is also no need for active contact.

People are able to experience the simultaneity of closeness and separation at such times and often permit themselves a floating that they would not ordinarily. My daughter, for instance, described a method that she developed for going to sleep at night. "When I can't sleep, I just stare at this one spot where the light comes in from the other houses through my shade," she told me. "I look at the patterns of light and try to keep from blinking. I hear you and Mom, and I know you are there but you feel far away. Sometimes I have thoughts and sometimes I don't, but eventually I just fall asleep." This kind of aloneness, proposed Winnicott, is the foundation of all creativity, since it is only in such a state that it is possible to explore one's internal world. The point is that it is not possible if one is *too* alone, or too intruded upon. It can only develop when the *holding* environment is safe and unobtrusive.

the capacity to be

Unintegration runs like a stream through almost thirty years of Winnicott's writings.[10] Beginning with a trickle (in a paper entitled *Primitive Emotional Development*), almost as an aside, it gathers force and intensity and ultimately cascades into all of the major themes of his work. The healthy individual is *not* always integrated, declared Winnicott in an early paper. In fact, it is *un*healthy to deny or to fear "the innate capacity of every human being to become unintegrated, depersonalized, and to feel that the world is unreal."[11]

As unintegration became more central to Winnicott's thinking, he began to tie it in more directly to his all-important notion of the "capacity to be." The infant who can *be,* as opposed to one who can only *do,* has the capacity to feel real.[12] In the unintegrated state, he makes discoveries about himself that affirm his sense of existing. Throughout a career that was always focused on how his patients felt unreal to themselves, Winnicott never tired of pointing out how that unreality stemmed from a parent's inability to leave a child alone without abandoning him.

My own sense of what unintegration might mean comes from a memory of what it was not. When I was five or six years old, my parents took me for swimming lessons to a local country club that we had just joined. A lifeguard took me into the pool and walked backward, across the length of it one or two steps beyond my reach while instructing me, "Swim to me, Mark. Swim to me." I did not know or particularly trust this fellow and had no sense (rightly or wrongly) of my parents' presence in the background. I did not want to swim to him, did not want his arms around me, and I gasped and struggled and cried. I refused all swimming lessons thereafter and taught myself primarily by holding my breath and going long distances underwater.

It was not until I was thirty years old, at a hotel pool on my honeymoon, that I realized I never exhaled underwater while I swam. Exhalation required a trust and a capacity to let go that I had not permitted myself. More recently, while on an intensive meditation retreat, I noticed a corollary of this experience. Concentrating with relative ease on the sensations of my in and out breaths, as I had been instructed, I began to notice a panicky feeling in the pit of my stomach every time I exhaled, before the start of the next breath. My final bit of exhalation was like a miniature unintegration: a dying into the next moment. It was not just in swimming that I was resisting this release.

Although Winnicott gave an occasional nod to spirituality or mysticism, his major emphasis was on the role of psychotherapy, play, or creativity (not necessarily in that order) in reestablishing the capacity to be. Knowing little of Buddhism, he could not appreciate how unabashedly it extols this state of unintegration. Understanding the defensive nature of most of our mental activity, the Buddha taught many methods of surrendering it. In my work as a therapist, I have adapted the Buddha's teachings to meet the needs of my patients, many of whom have no time or interest in formal meditation practice.

A patient of mine, for example, a twenty-eight-year-old actress from Texas named Lucy, came to consult with me after a series of workshops with her voice teacher. Lucy was a very accomplished woman: confident, verbal, and engaging, but tense and rather critical of herself. Her teacher was an imposing man in his mid-fifties who ran his workshops with a combination of lighthearted ease and demanding attention to detail. Lucy's earliest childhood memory was of hiding from her parents' drunken fighting. She had had little of the nondemanding support that Winnicott saw as essential for the capacity to be and had instead developed the responsible and cerebral persona that often grows out of a child's early attempts to cope with parental unhappiness. Feeling both threatened by unhappiness and responsible for it, Lucy had learned how to hold herself together to manage her parents' moods. Now in her late twenties, she was beginning to see how her tenseness and criticalness tended to interfere with her ability to enter into her characters' roles.

Lucy came to me because her interactions with her voice teacher were making her very uncomfortable. She felt that she was entering "the lion's den" every time she went to see him. He was giving her exercises to do that demanded that she sing freely in front of him, and he was interrupting her every time he detected a note of falseness in her voice. She was experiencing her teacher as if he were the brutal, raging father of her youth, and she found herself becoming fearful, anxious, and angry every time she had to see him alone. Needless to say, her performances were getting worse instead of better.

Lucy came to me because she could not figure out how to relate freely to her teacher. She knew what she had to do, but she could not find a way to get past her anxiety. She alternated between being cool, composed, and cerebral, trying to "figure out" what to do, and feeling utterly dejected while crying uninterruptedly in the bathroom, imagining that her career was over. She could hold herself together or fall apart, but she could not do the third thing: She could not go into the lion's den and relate honestly, just as I could not exhale underwater.

Lucy was experiencing a major obstacle to unintegration: anticipation of the past. She was laying the transparency of her history over the present situation just as a lecturer does with an overhead projector and a screen. Assessing the situation with her rational mind and fearing the dangers of the past, she was preventing herself from having any kind of new, and unantici- pated, experience.

I explained to Lucy that in the history of Buddhism the fierce local deities of tribal or animistic cultures were always converted into protectors of the Buddhist way. Her task, as I saw it, was to ask the lion's collaboration, to turn the internal- ized remnant of her abusive father into a protector of the Dharma (or truth). She could not manage, nor ignore, her projections; she had to learn to be with them. Permitting her teacher to be her brutal, raging, lionlike father, and relating to him as such, was the first step in allowing herself to go to pieces. I suggested that she had to befriend the lion. Perhaps she could bring him some milk.

My thinking in giving such advice was that Lucy's raging father was blocking her access to her spontaneous voice. He was a big obstacle, and Lucy needed to engage him. The teacher had taken on some of her father's qualities, and Lucy had to make use of that in order to proceed. By allowing him to be the lion, she could use her relationship to find her way around all that her father's anger had done to her.

Lucy was afraid to stop holding herself together. She was worried that she would be flooded by terrifying feelings of abandonment, or by the immensity of her parents' unhappiness. In some way, I believe, she was afraid that if she let herself go, she would be letting her parents go, that in keeping herself together she was protecting them or her connection to them. But the price she was paying was to be perpetually wound up. "We are poor indeed," said Winnicott in a famous footnote, "if we are only sane."[13] For Lucy to sing meant stopping the mind that had once protected her.

Lucy's task was to reestablish contact with her capacity for unintegration, to heal the split between her coping self and the silent center of her personality. She was reaching for an intensity and an intimacy that is lacking when the thinking mind is always trying to maintain control. Although she did not literally take my advice to leave her teacher some milk, she did gain the lion's collaboration. By not hiding from her fear, she was able to actually engage with him. She sang her first notes in the quavering voice of a little girl and was relieved to find that her teacher did not make fun of her. As in Joseph Goldstein's encounter with the Zen master, her teacher seemed to respond to the authenticity of her approach. He helped her to reclaim the power that she had ceded to her abusive father long ago.

freedom from the known

Just as Lucy had to find a way to shake herself free from the defensive rigidity of her reactions to her father's rage, so do most of us have to free ourselves from overlearned responses that become habitual and restrictive. Another patient of mine, a therapist in her own right, had a dream that seemed to open up this possibility for her. Maryanne dreamed of a musical conductor, a tweedy sort of man, who was very busy with his musical scores and with a number of people in his room.

"What I want from you," Maryanne remembered saying in the dream, "is to turn down the noise."

I took this as a direct message to me and told her so. Maryanne had a way of filling the space in the room with talk. She was rarely silent and rarely permitted me the spacious silence that I was used to settling into while working. As a therapist, she had theories about almost everything that she brought up, and sometimes even theories about the theories. Yet here she was, wanting me to turn down the cacophony. Could the noise in her dream be the noise of her own mind, I wondered? Was she compulsively engaged in "needing to know" all of the time?

"Do you know what?" she asked. "My mother would always say to me dismissively, 'What do *you* know?'"

As a child, Maryanne was always having to prove to her mother that she did, in fact, know something. She was never allowed, nor could she now allow herself, to have a mind that was unencumbered by knowing.

In the Tibetan tradition of Buddhism, those moments of unknowing when the mind is naturally loosed from its moorings are said to be special opportunities for realization. During orgasm, at the moment of death, or while falling asleep or ending a dream are times when the veils of knowing are spontaneously lifted and the underlying luminosity of the mind shines through. But we have a powerful resistance to experiencing this mind in all of its brilliance. We are afraid to let ourselves go all the way. To set ourselves adrift requires a trust that for most of us was lost in childhood. To Maryanne, it seemed more important to keep proving herself to her long deceased mother than it was to find some peace and quiet in her own mind. Only very gradually could she learn to turn down her own noise, and she was delighted when there were no terrible repercussions.

One of the most important tasks of adulthood is to discover, or rediscover, the ability to lose oneself. To do this we must understand the difference between unintegration and disintegration. The Chinese expression for orgasm, *"having a high tide,"* describes this difference quite effectively. In a high tide everything is floating, the self is submerged or dissolved, there is no longer any foothold or point of reference, but it is not chaos. When we are afraid to relax the mind's vigilance, however, we tend to equate this floating with drowning and we start to founder. In this fear, we destroy our capacity to discover ourselves in a new way. We doom ourselves to a perpetual hardening of character, which we imagine is sanity but which comes to imprison us. Our shoulders get more and more tense.

Just the other day I had a vivid experience of how conditioned my everyday mind is by this vigilance. It was early on a Saturday morning, and I had to go to our parking garage to get my car to take my son to his 10:00 A.M. soccer game. I left the house by 9:30, got to the garage at 9:40, and found that the car wouldn't start. The attendant took out jumper cables, moved another car nearby, connected the cables, and tried to jump the battery. My lights had been left on, it turned out, and the battery needed about five minutes before it would charge enough to start up. I kept looking at my watch, congratulating myself on how balanced and in the moment I was remaining, doing one thing after the other without getting aggravated while still having the chance of making it to my son's game in time. One thing was just flowing into the next, and my mind was at ease. I reset the electric clock in my car as I drove to pick up my family and ushered them in with time to spare.

"What took you so long?" they asked immediately.

I told them, rather proudly, and pointed to the clock to show them how we would still make it to the game.

"That's not the time," they said. "It's already 10:15!"

I argued for a split second and then realized, with sudden alarm, that the car battery was not the only one to have run down. The battery in my watch was also dying. I had sailed so effortlessly through this series of events because my neurotic attachment to time had been momentarily loosened. Released from the grip of time, my caretaker self had relaxed, and my mind had risen to the occasion and attended to what needed to be done.

In a similar way in both therapy and meditation, when the tyrannical influence of the compensatory mind is temporarily lifted, a window is opened into unintegration. Then, like a child who is not afraid to be left alone, we are free to have a new experience. It is a paradox of self-discovery that we can know ourselves only by surrendering into the void.

p a r t   t w o

SMILING

f i n d i n g   a   p r a c t i c e

Be patient, do nothing, cease striving. We find this advice disheartening and therefore unfeasible because we forget it is our own inflexible activity that is structuring the reality. We think that if we do not hustle, nothing will happen and we will pine away. But the reality is probably in motion and after a while we *might* take part in that motion. But one can't know.

PAUL GOODMAN [1]

3
m e d i t a t i o n

There is an expression in horseback riding circles that one is supposed to ride with "soft eyes," letting the world go by without focusing on any one thing too specifically. I learned about it from a patient who was having a problem doing complicated jumps with her horse, but I was interested in the broader applications of what she discovered. My patient, a young woman named Marilyn, was an accomplished rider, but, as she described it, she was "too involved" when it came to mastering a new set of hurdles. She was too focused on achievement, she told me, to permit her "soft eyes" to develop. Unable to relax into the jump, her tension and her desire for success interfered with the horse's capacity to navigate the obstacles cleanly. Like an actor stumbling over her lines, Marilyn grew more and more unsure of herself, and her performance became more and more self-conscious.

One of her riding instructors showed Marilyn a way to distract herself from her worried anticipation. He urged her to imagine that an additional turn took place after the final leap. He gave her a method of getting her mind out of the way. This mental trick worked beautifully. Rather than becoming fixated on the jump as the culmination of her efforts, Marilyn was able to set the jump up and then move on. As she was visualizing the imaginary turn, her horse soared perfectly into the air. Because her mind was at ease, Marilyn was able to sit back and enjoy the fruits of her efforts.

As Marilyn told me her story, I realized that she had been resisting that critical moment when her self fell away, when she and the horse and the jump became one. By worrying over how well she was doing, she was perpetuating the hold of her ego, refusing to allow it to fade back into transparency. Her ambition had been interfering with her success. Her riding instructor's efforts to show Marilyn her "soft eyes" were attempts to bring forward her capacity for unintegration, to allow her to surrender into the connection with her horse that the jump demanded. What was interesting was that Marilyn needed a trick to make this natural thing happen. Telling her to have "soft eyes" was not enough; she needed something to do with her mind to get it out of the way. This is the function of meditation practice: It provides a method of getting the mind out of the way so that we can be at one with our experience.

While I have never been much of a horseback rider, I could relate to Marilyn's predicament, and to her solution. When I was in elementary school, I developed something of a stammer, especially when I had to introduce myself or say my own name. My anticipation of having to speak, like Marilyn's anticipation of having to jump, created such a reaction within me that I became immobilized. My parents finally took me to a speech therapist, a kindly gray-haired woman named Mrs. Stanton whose musty office I remember was up a long and dusty flight of stairs in downtown New Haven. We played board games, which I enjoyed, and while we played we would talk. She told me once about a man with a stutter who had a particularly difficult time with words that began with the letter *w*. He would always have trouble when he had to introduce his wife at a party. I remember laughing together, with some horror on my part, over the plight of this poor gentleman, struggling to introduce his w-w-w-wife. In the midst of these games and discussions, Mrs. Stanton taught me how to distract myself when the stammering was imminent. By stamping my foot lightly, or touching the table in front of me, I could create enough space for the words to come. Just as Marilyn had learned how to get out of the way so that she could jump, I learned how to let go so that I could speak.

Years later, when I would get stuck in a therapy session, my therapist would urge much the same strategy. "Speak without thinking," he would tell me. I was always surprised to find that I would say just the right thing. The lesson was similar. Speech does not always have to be thought out beforehand. We discover what we need to say when we get out of the way of ourselves.

Recently, I was sitting in my office with a young woman named Cara who began to tell me of an affair she was beginning with a married man.

"I know you won't believe me," she said, "but he's a nice guy. He loves his wife. What he's doing having an affair with me if he loves his wife, I can't tell you, but he seems different from other married men I've been involved with."

While successful in her work life, Cara could be intensely self-critical and insecure in her personal life. I had long puzzled over what had kept her from getting involved with someone she could really be with. As we talked about the married man and how he was "different," I began to see that Cara was put at ease by how much this man cared for his wife. She had none of the usual anxiety or insecurity that accompanied discussions of other potential lovers or suitors.

"You seem to like the fact that he is so fond of his wife," I ventured.

"I do?" she responded, surprised. "Why do you say that?"

"You're not obsessing over whether he likes you or not," I pointed out.

In her own way, Cara had stumbled upon the trick of Marilyn's riding instructor and my speech therapist. She had found a way to relax her obsessing mind so that she could start to feel what it was like to be with someone without being overwhelmed by her own anxiety. In fact, what she confided to me about her last rendezvous was that the part she had enjoyed the most was coming home from work and getting herself ready to meet him. The anticipation was actually exciting. She enjoyed the preparations without turning them into an orgy of insecurity.

As is often the case in psychotherapy, symptoms contain a hint of their cure. It would have been all too easy to see Cara's affair as simply another example of her attraction to unavailable men, and to leave it at that. Yet for Cara, the issue was much more about how she repeatedly made *herself* unapproachable by wondering obsessively whether a boyfriend liked her or not. Only by distracting herself from these thoughts could she learn what it meant to make herself available to someone. Only then could she discover, as Marilyn had, that it was possible to enjoy those moments of connection in which the day-to-day self drops away. In times such as this, we need to learn how to immobilize our reactive and anticipatory minds so that we can make the connections we are seeking.

In Buddhism, there is a similar understanding and a very

specific approach to bringing about these kinds of connections. If we feel empty, taught the Buddha, we must not let that emptiness paralyze us. If we are reaching for intimacy, we must let ourselves get out of the way. If we want peace, we must first learn how to quiet our own minds. If we want release, we must learn how to cease our own craving.

There is a famous story about one of the Buddha's early followers, the bandit Angulimala, that drives home the Buddha's most fundamental teaching. One of the most feared criminals of the Buddha's time, Angulimala distinguished himself by his habit of garlanding himself with the severed fingers of his murdered victims. When word got out that he and his band were in a certain area of the countryside, all who could possibly avoid travelling in that area would do so. The Buddha's followers naturally beseeched their teacher not to make himself vulnerable to the bandit, but he obstinately refused to capitulate to their warnings and set out on the country roads that led toward the murderer's turf. On seeing the Buddha from afar, Angulimala armed himself and began to follow the holy man. But the Buddha, through his extraordinary powers, made it impossible for Angulimala to catch up with him no matter how strenuously he was pursued. Exasperated, Angulimala paused and shouted out, "Stop, recluse! Stop!"

Although the Buddha continued to walk, he shouted back paradoxically, "I have stopped, Angulimala, you stop too."

Puzzled, Angulimala gave his famous response: "While you

are walking, you tell me you have stopped, but now, when I have stopped, you say I have not stopped. I ask you now about the meaning: How is it that you have stopped and I have not?"[2]

The Buddha's intervention momentarily interrupted Angulimala. He got the murderer's attention, looked deeply into his eyes, and explained to him that he had stopped creating suffering for himself. Elaborating his teachings to Angulimala, he converted him from one of the most feared outlaws of his time to one of his most accomplished followers.

Just as I had to learn to stop my worry rather than my speech, so did Angulimala have to learn to stop more than just his locomotion. The great problem with our minds, as with our selves, the Buddha explained, is how to stop them. We must learn to relax the grip of the thinking mind that is always, like Angulimala, assessing its next victim.

avoiding contact

As a student of human neurosis, Freud was familiar with the mind's tendency to interfere with its own satisfaction. In his own way he understood something of what the Buddha explained to Angulimala. In his descriptions of the obsessional character, for example, he gave great credence to the power of the mind to interrupt the flow of gratifying experience. He called this a psychological defense and gave it the name *isolat-*

ing. Speaking primarily in sexual terms, Freud described how the thinking mind interferes with experience and removes the possibility of successful contact. Erotic experience depends on the ego's striving to become one with that which it desires, Freud recognized,[3] but this is also a potent source of anxiety. We fear that which we most desire, the falling away of self that accompanies a powerful connection. In a moment of successful contact, as in Marilyn's jump, my spontaneous speech, or Cara's unself-conscious exchange with her lover, there is a brief but exuberant unity, a touching or a connection in which we forget ourselves and are enriched. Our selves are reconfigured in this process. But Freud was witness to how people restrict this capacity by holding themselves back. It is as if we have a "taboo on touching,"[4] he said.

Our everyday thinking minds are obsessional in exactly this way. The thinking mind remembers itself constantly, not wanting to forget or to be forgotten. It must always have something to do. Like an ever-vigilant, overly intrusive chaperone, it interrupts any possibility of connection. As Freud described it, the thinking mind prohibits contact by "interpolating an interval"[5] whenever and wherever it is possible. A patient of mine, for instance, had trouble at times reading a paragraph without saying the words "comma" or "period" to herself when she came upon these marks in her books. She felt compelled to interrupt herself at every opportunity. In a less dramatic but more far-reaching way, our endlessly repetitive thinking interferes with our ability to connect with our own world. Isolated in our heads, we yearn for the kind of connection that our own thinking guards against.

In murdering victim after victim, Angulimala was acting out this obsessional pattern of punctuation, compulsively interpolating intervals into his experience by repeatedly extinguishing life. In a less obvious way, but by using similar mechanisms, our own endless and repetitive thoughts squeeze the life out of life, vigilantly guarding against the loss of self that we fear.

One of the most profound aspects of intensive meditation practice is that it throws us up against this very phenomenon. The sheer volume of pointless thinking that is going on inside our heads becomes inescapable in the quiet of meditation. For many people, this comes as quite a shock. We are used to thinking of thinking as a good thing, as that which makes us human. It can be quite a revelation to discover that so much of our thinking appears to be boring, repetitive, and pointless while keeping us isolated and cut off from the feelings of connection that we most value. This was precisely the experience of a patient of mine, a composer named Kelly, who on her first nine-day retreat was incredulous at the sheer quantity of obsessing, worrying, and planning in her mind.

"If I had only put a fraction of the time spent worrying into my work, I would have gotten so much done in my life!" she exclaimed in our first session after the retreat.

"What was all that obsessing defending against?" I wondered.

"Engagement," she said quickly.

"And why should engagement be frightening?" I puzzled.

"Disappointment in the actuality of the experience," she answered, after only a brief hesitation.

Rather than risking an encounter that might not meet her expectations, Kelly held herself aloof in her mind, recoiling from an imagined disappointment. As our discussions continued, Kelly came to see that she was similarly avoiding any intimate relationship that had the least hint of ambivalence. She had no trouble concocting enormous crushes on idealized figures whom she then avoided, but the fear of disappointment prevented her from engaging with anyone for whom she could foresee ambivalent feelings. In the aftermath of her meditation experience, Kelly began to see that by quieting her own mind she could find a middle way between idealization and isolation by venturing more willingly into relationships that carried the potential for disappointment. By not "buying in" to the chatter of her own mind, Kelly learned that she did not have to be so isolated. The chatter was a form of protection from being touched, but it was a protection that had its own side effects. Kelly could take more risks and make more contact than she thought.

Psychotherapy has long been aware of the defensive nature of much of our day-to-day thinking and has striven to find ways of undermining its tenacious hold over our minds. Once Freud figured out that the purpose of so much of our thinking is to isolate us from the flow of gratifying experience, he began to see this dynamic in many of his friends and patients. Much of the liberating promise of early psychoanalysis stemmed from its attempts to cure this isolating tendency of the human mind. But scattered within Freud's writings we find references to his frustrations in actually effecting the kinds of changes he was reaching for. He thought deeply about the reasons for the self-imposed isolation of the thinking mind but had difficulty translating his insights into a method of change. While his insights were revelatory, he did not have the method of the Buddha within his grasp.

being-time

In a short, masterful, and little discussed paper written in 1915 called "On Transience," Freud reached for a fearless mental posture that unknowingly paralleled that of the Buddha while at the same time offering a parable about the limitations of his analytic method. Recounting a summer walk that he took through a "smiling countryside" with a "taciturn" friend and a "young but already famous poet," Freud described how his friends were unable to smile back at the beauty that surrounded them. They could admire the sights, he observed, but they could not *feel*. They were locked into their own minds, unwilling or unable to surrender to the beauty surrounding them. Like Kelly on her first retreat, but without her self-awareness, they were unconsciously guarding themselves against engagement with something that might disappoint them.

"The proneness to decay of all that is beautiful and perfect can, as we know, give rise to two different impulses in the mind," wrote Freud at the beginning of this essay. "The one leads to the aching despondency felt by the young poet, while the other leads to rebellion against the fact asserted."[6] Either we get depressed when confronted with impermanence, suggested Freud, or we devalue what we see and push it away. Just as Freud described these two possible reactions, so did the Buddha. He called them attachment and aversion, although Freud's terms of "aching despondency" and "rebellion against the facts" would have done just as well.

Only by cultivating a mind that does neither, taught the Buddha, can transience become enlightening. This is, in fact, the heart of the Buddha's teaching: that it is possible to cultivate a mind that neither clings nor rejects, and that in so doing we can alter the way in which we experience both time and our selves.

Like the Buddha, Freud did not want to yield to either of the two alternatives of attachment or aversion. He was seeking a third option but had trouble finding the words to describe what it could be. Like a Japanese Zen master whose full attention is focused on the sound of the crickets or the taste of a strawberry, Freud sought to return his friends to a more intimate and immediate experience of the moment. "It was incomprehensible, I declared, that the thought of the transience of beauty should interfere with our joy in it. . . . A flower that blossoms only for a single night does not seem to us on that account less lovely."[7] Yet Freud's exhortations did not move his friends. He was unable to open their senses to the beauty surrounding them. Their hearts remained closed, their minds stubbornly disconnected from their bodies, their avoidance of transience overshadowing their sights, smells, and perceptions.

Why, asked Freud, do we prevent the flow in moments such as these? Why do we hold ourselves back from contact? Why do we hold ourselves so aloof? His friends' disengagement on their summer walk obviously had all kinds of reverberations. Would they not hold themselves back from love just as they were holding themselves back from nature?

In Freud's discussion of his two friends' hard-heartedness, he had the realization that they were trying to fend off an inevitable mourning. In their obsessional way, they were isolating themselves and refusing to be touched. His description is powerful because it mirrors each of our refusal to embrace the transience of all that is important to us, including our own selves. To one degree or another, we are all, like his friends, in a state of abbreviated, or interrupted, mourning. Acutely aware of our own transience, we alternate between an aching despondency and a rebellion against the facts. We cling to our loved ones, or remove ourselves from them, rather than loving them in all of their vulnerability. In so doing we distance ourselves from a grief that is an inevitable component of affection. Using our best obsessional defenses to keep this mourning at bay, we pay a price in how isolated and cut off we can feel.

There is a well-known Buddhist story: A Tibetan master's son died suddenly from illness. Hearing him weep inconsolably, the master's disciples came and confronted him with their surprise. "You taught us that all is illusion and that we should not be attached," they admonished him. "Why are you weeping and wailing?"

The master answered immediately, "Indeed, all is illusion. But the loss of a child is the most painful illusion."

The master did not attempt to inhibit his attachment or his mourning. He was able to embrace grief as wholeheartedly as beauty. By pushing away the painful aspect of experience, Freud observed, his friends were isolating themselves from their own capacity for love. As the Tibetan master's reaction made clear, love and grieving, like separation and connection, are co-constitutive. Opening oneself to one emotion deepens the experience of the other. The heart can open in sadness as much as it does in joy.

In the Buddha's teachings on transience, his point is that

everything is *always* changing. When we take loved objects into our egos with the hope or expectation of having them forever, we are deluding ourselves and postponing an inevitable grief. The solution is not to deny attachment but to become less controlling in how we love. From a Buddhist perspective, it is the very tendency to protect ourselves against mourning that is the cause of the greatest dissatisfaction. As the great thirteenth-century Japanese Zen master Dogen wrote in his discussion of what he called "being-time," it is possible to have a relationship to transience that is not adversarial, in which the ability to embrace the moment takes precedence over fear of its passing.

"Do not regard time as merely flying away," he warned. "Do not think flying away is its sole function. For time to fly away there would have to be a separation (between it and things). Because you imagine that time only passes, you do not learn the truth. . . ."[8] What Dogen was saying was that we are not actually separate from time. When we distance ourselves and recoil from time's passing, we are creating an artificial duality. Our being and time are not separate, they are one and the same. They are all we have.

Much of our endless and repetitive thinking is functioning to distance us from this realization. Isolated in our own heads, we avoid the window into impermanence that intimate connection provides. The Buddha observed that the mind has the tendency to cling or to recoil in such circumstances but the capacity to do neither. Meditation is a way of learning how to permit the temporary intermingling that makes an intimate connection possible. Freud understood how necessary this intermingling could be but had trouble finding a way to make it accessible for his friends. Buddha devoted his forty years of teaching to showing how the practice of meditation could open up this capacity for anyone.

tricking the mind

In Buddhism, breaking through the thinking mind's isolation requires something other than just analysis. It requires a new way of being with the mind, one in which its observing functions take precedence over its reactive ones. It is a way of resurrecting that benign silence of the mother who can watch without interfering in her child's play. The Buddha taught how to use meditation as a vehicle for putting worry and self-consciousness on hold, just as Mrs. Stanton taught me to distract myself from my anxiety. Substituting a more benign caretaker, a watcher or observer, for the split-off mental functioning of the obsessively thinking mind, meditation tricks the self the way Marilyn's instructor tricked her into allowing her horse to jump.

Viewed in this manner, there is something homeopathic about the Buddha's medicine of meditation. It takes a little bit of the symptom and uses it to cure the bigger problem. As I became more and more familiar with the core meditative strategy of moment-to-moment awareness that runs like a thread through the different kinds of Buddhism, I was struck by the many obsessive features that this practice has. This technique, which goes by the name of mindfulness or bare attention, requires the careful noting of everything that occurs in the mind-body spectrum as it unfolds. The meditator is taught, for example, to distinguish the lifting, moving, and placing motions of the foot as she walks, or the chewing, tasting, and swallowing sensations as she eats. Emotional reactions of liking or disliking are not repressed, but are carefully noted as responses that are distinguishable from the core events. Successful practice requires both distancing—in the setting up of a "watcher"—and interruption of the flow of experience—through the noting of its component parts.

When I learned to practice mindfulness, I was taught to keep up a running commentary on my own process in the form of an ongoing labelling: "Lifting the arm, grasping the fork, moving it toward the mouth, opening the mouth, hungry, hungry, smelling the food, remembering the last time I had this, hoping it's good, feeling the warmth of the food, too hot, tasting the food, disappointment, disappointment, hearing a noise, chewing, chewing, feeling saliva, swallowing, wanting more." In a retreat, this kind of self-observation continues throughout very long days. As I learned to separate my emotional reactions from my sensory experience, my mind began to settle down. It became, not unresponsive, but much less reactive. Similar in tone to a mother who can be simultaneously holding but not intrusive, this noting mind gently coaxed me toward an experience of how transient *everything* is. This witnessing is the most common beginning strategy in meditation: It permits a subtle alternative to the obsessive distancing that Freud described so beautifully in his friends.

The interesting thing about meditation is how disposable it is. It has no need to outlive its own usefulness and is ultimately expendable. In the progress of meditation, for example, as detailed in any number of Buddhist psychological texts, the witness is always eventually dropped. The sense of duality that Dogen targeted in his discussions of "being-time" falls away. Many a meditator labors for long periods before listening carefully to the voice of her teacher, yet the message is always the same. The ego, be it the thinking mind or even the observing self, is eventually quieted, releasing us into a profound connection.

One of my favorite stories, from the early days of Zen Buddhism in China, gives the same message. An accomplished meditator, a monk named Ma-tsu, was sitting diligently at his monastery in a long retreat. His master went to him one day and asked him, "Virtuous one, for what purpose are you sitting in meditation?"

"I wish to become a Buddha," answered the monk.

Upon hearing this answer the master picked up a loose tile and began rubbing it on a stone in front of the monastery.

"What are you doing?" asked the monk with alarm.

"I am polishing this tile to make a mirror," answered the master.

"How can you make a mirror by polishing a tile?" exclaimed Ma-tsu.

"And how can you make a Buddha by practicing *zazen* (meditation)?" returned the master.[9]

As the story makes clear, meditation involves a kind of co-opting of the obsessive mind, replacing it with an ever-more-subtle version of itself that must eventually be surrendered completely, releasing the meditator into the terror and delight of pure expression. The monk, while a sincere and diligent meditator, was still engaged in the obsessive act of polishing. His master, with the clarity of vision that is always attributed to the realized beings of these stories, could see that the witnessing had done its work. His student was ready to drop the caretaking function of the observer altogether.

The beauty of meditation practice is that it provides a continuous and ever-deepening method of closing in on the isolating tendency of the thinking mind. "The old ego dies hard," observed the playwright Samuel Beckett, "such as it was, a minister of dullness, it was also an agent of security."[10] In replacing one agent of security with another less obtrusive one, meditation empowers the observing mind while relieving some of the ego's enforced dullness. At a certain point, the meditator, ready for a true embrace, takes what one Zen master called the "backward step" and jettisons the observer altogether.

This progression, from isolation and distancing to intimacy and connection, is one that characterizes the Buddhist path in all of its manifestations. The practice of meditation, through its empowering of the observing mind and its refusal to adhere to the two alternatives of attachment and aversion, is the crucial link between the two. It is a practice that permits a method of being in harmony with the transience of the world without succumbing to its oppressiveness.

embracing impermanence

I had a very personal reminder of this not so long ago when my wife and I ran into the rabbi who had performed our wedding ceremony fourteen years earlier. We had sought out this rabbi because of his interest in Jewish mystical teachings and his sympathy toward Buddhism. He had performed a lovely ceremony which had culminated in the traditional breaking of a wine glass underfoot. As he introduced this part of the ritual, the rabbi spoke of how stomping on the glass symbolized the stamping out of emptiness and the filling of life with love.

"Stamping out emptiness?" my Buddhist friends kidded me after the ceremony. "How do we do that?"

When I ran into this rabbi at a friend's art opening many years later, he related how he had become more and more interested in Buddhism in the intervening years. First he had started to meditate, he told me, feeling that it might help him to relax or to become less tense and neurotic. "Instead, it blew me apart," he acknowledged. Intrigued and puzzled, he began to pursue a more rigorous study of Buddhism.

I related to him how my Buddhist friends had remarked on his attempts to stamp out emptiness and asked him if his ideas had changed at all. "Now when I do a wedding," he said, smiling a little sheepishly, "I don't talk about smashing emptiness but about embracing it." Breaking the glass, for my rabbi, had come to mean accepting the transitory nature of all things. Intimacy puts us in touch with fragility, he realized, and the acceptance of fragility opens us to intimacy. Even in a wedding ceremony that is a celebration of union, there is an undercurrent of mourning over impermanence. Revelling in intimacy means simultaneously appreciating its fleetingness. This is one of the reasons why we shy away from intimacy—it tends to put us in touch with our own vulnerability.

In Freud's walk through the countryside the issue was also about appreciating the connection between beauty and fragility. The psychoanalyst in Freud was able to understand why his friends would not relax their vigilance, but he was powerless to get them to stop. He did not have the ability that the Buddha demonstrated in his exchange with the murderer Angulimala, nor did he have the confidence that it was possible to break through the obsessive distancing that his friends personified. Most of us exist in a state similar to that of Freud's friends. Our minds are running on without us, keeping us at a distance from that which we love, or from love itself. We justifiably complain of feeling unreal because we are busy keeping ourselves at arm's length from the biggest reality of all—the transience of which we are a part. Rather than permitting a flow, we impose an interruption that interferes with satisfaction or fulfillment. As my rabbi discovered, successfully permitting an intimate connection requires the ability to embrace impermanence. The flower that blooms for only a single night is indeed a sight to behold.

4
connection

It is no surprise to me that the Tibetan Buddhist tradition uses the passion of an intimate relationship as a metaphor for the spiritual journey since both seek to satisfy very similar longings. People look to their lovers for a feeling of connection much as they look to their spiritual pursuits for meaning in their lives. The reverberations of a mutual attraction are parallel in some ways to the discovery of the power of meditation. Both involve a momentary surrender to something greater than one's usual self.

In my experience as a therapist I have found that the yearning for this kind of connection is one of the most common reasons for people to seek therapy. They wonder what they are doing wrong, why they cannot find happiness in their intimate lives, or why they cannot find a lover. They worry over their ability to love or be loved. There is a feeling of desperation coupled with a sense of unworthiness. People in this predicament will say things to me like, "I know I cannot love another person until I can love myself," looking for some remedy to fix the problem. I always tell them to forget about that one, that they are thinking about connection backwards. Who are we loving when we profess to love ourselves, anyway?

The major obstacle to love, I have found, is a premature walling off of the personality that results in a falseness or inauthenticity that other people can feel. Love, after all, requires a person to be open and vulnerable, able to tolerate and enjoy the crossing of ego boundaries that occurs naturally under the spell of passion. As Joseph Goldstein found in his encounter with the Zen master, when he became vulnerable, there was a spontaneous moment of heart touching heart. When someone is so uncomfortable with his own sense of emptiness that he struggles to keep it at bay, there is no way he will be able to be open with another person. He will simply be too ashamed to reveal himself in any real manner. Therapy is effective in this kind of situation when it allows a person to discover his or her own capacity for connection. As my friend the psychoanalyst and writer Michael Eigen has written, "The hallmark of the therapeutic session is the discovery of intimacy in the face of unflinching aloneness."[1]

While this kind of problem is often what brings people into

therapy, it is also a common precipitant for the spiritual search and is something that the spiritual traditions address in their own way. By giving people the *means* of being themselves, no matter what kind of vulnerability they are bearing, meditation prepares the ground for intimacy. By teaching people how to be less self-conscious, and more accepting, of their own idiosyncrasies, meditation clears away some of the defensive rigidity that obscures the natural flow of love.

When plagued with a sense of unworthiness, it is easy to feel deficient and to see the love of another person as the only possible solution to one's plight. Meditation tends to work against this assumption of deficiency by restoring the capacity for connection from the inside. It is like a stealth bomber that sneaks through all the defenses and illuminates the central fortress of the heart. In doing this, it challenges the common assumption of our culture about where connection comes from. In the Buddhist view, connection is already present. We are not as separate and distinct as we think we are. Connection is our natural state; we just have to learn to permit it.

learning to be

One of the first people to make me aware of this peculiar truth was a former Harvard University psychology professor named Richard Alpert, who was, by the mid-seventies, known by his assumed name of Ram Dass. No longer teaching within the ivy-covered walls of academia, Ram Dass was nevertheless a pivotal figure during my early years at Harvard. He had returned from a spiritual odyssey to India, was years removed from his initial excitement over the use of LSD, and was instrumental in carrying the wisdom of the East to the generation that came of age during the Vietnam War.

Straddling the fence between therapist and guru, he made himself available for privately scheduled interviews, structured much like a therapist's, to whoever approached him for counsel. I went to see Ram Dass shortly after my brief initial flirtation with therapy in college, full of many of the same questions and feelings that had provoked my earlier attempt to seek help. I met with him in Boulder, Colorado, where I had gone to begin my explorations of Buddhism. Although my primary motivation, in my private meeting with him, was the desire for a meaningful relationship, I also secretly hoped that he would be able to help me heal my private sense of unworthiness.

As soon as I entered Ram Dass's room, I realized that this was to be unlike any therapeutic encounter that I might have imagined. After the briefest of hellos, Ram Dass began to gaze at me unceasingly, looking straight into my eyes but at the same time looking past me. He seemed filled with love but also completely uninterested in me, or at least in who I thought I was. He did not respond to any of my smiles, nods, or grimaces, or to any of my attempts to engage or avoid him. He simply waited, gazing at me with an unnerving and unwavering intensity that I could not quite understand. I felt perplexed yet realized that there was nothing much I could do. I tried to explain what I wanted from him: some inspiration, some guidance, some help in feeling better about myself so that I could find a girlfriend. But he seemed remarkably unmoved by my words and just continued moving his head ever so slightly back and forth while occasionally making a soft sound like, "Ahhhh."

When I had said everything I could think of, I settled into a kind of uneasy silence in which a variety of images, memories, thoughts, and anxieties floated by. Anger, self-consciousness, and shame all took turns in my mind. I had entered the realm of the Freudian unconscious. But even this did not interest Ram Dass in particular. He seemed infinitely patient and subtly encouraging, as if beckoning to me from afar.

"What was this man *doing*?" I wondered to myself. "How should I react?"

But no matter what I tried, Ram Dass did not budge. Finally, out of desperation and unable to think of anything else to think about, I began to return his gaze. This was suddenly very different. Finding myself in a place beyond words, I actually felt a connection with him and sensed a moment of mutual recognition. And then all of a sudden, I realized the answer to my question. Ram Dass was not *doing* anything, which is why my attempts to figure out what he wanted were not moving him. He was simply being. I was going through all kinds of internal gyrations, but he was simply being. Although I was mobilized to feel *done to*, that was not what was happening. I was being given room to *be* and out of that experience was discovering that we could be together.

After several minutes of this connecting, which was actually very moving for me, Ram Dass broke the silence with a few words of his own.

"Are you in there?" he asked. "I'm in here," he added, pointing to himself.

Then, smiling, he said in the vernacular of the day, "Far out."

This kind of connection was a new experience for me, and one that actually answered most of what had motivated me to seek him out in the first place. I was concerned about my ability to love and would have done whatever reasonably sounding thing a therapist would have suggested I do to uncover why I could not love. But my session with Ram Dass saved me from that. In our brief time together he made a big impression, showing me that I was capable of more than I thought, that my separateness did not negate the possibility of connection, and that love sprung from the capacity to be. Seeing myself as someone "in need" began to yield to an entirely different experience, one in which my capacity for plenitude revealed itself.

In making himself available to me, Ram Dass simply drew me out beyond my own self-consciousness to a place where I was still separate but was also connected. My defensive self dropped away, and I was left in unknown territory, where all of my ideas about myself were open to question. The connection that I was seeking was already here. I did not need to seek it outside of myself as much as I needed to open to my own ability to just be. I departed feeling restored, with Ram Dass encouraging me to remember that this capacity was available to me in my regular life. In his own way, he was revealing an essential and paradoxical truth: Separation and connectedness exist simultaneously and make each other possible. At the same time that I was in here and he was over there, we were also at one.

There was nothing in Ram Dass's method that would have been shocking to an experienced psychotherapist, except perhaps the intensity of his gaze. In my brief encounter with him, I ran through, in abbreviated form, much of the material of conventional psychotherapy while arriving, however briefly, at a place of connection that had seemed completely out of reach.

I became aware while sitting with him of how contracted I was in my day-to-day personality, of how eager I was to please, and of how insecure I felt about my ability to do that successfully. I could see how contracting made me feel empty, not quite real, and not whole, because, in fact, I was only being a fraction of myself. Only by letting go, on the one side, and opening, on the other, could I become *more* real by becoming *less* known to myself. Only by relaxing my mind, moving *away* from my usual thinking and into awareness, could I find the realm behind the id.

Ram Dass was giving me an opportunity, however briefly, to touch the ground of my being, to break a path through my self to the realm behind personal identity and the unconscious. Love did not depend on how together I felt, nor was it something that I had to *do*. It was the more natural state, one that I had to learn how to permit.

Buddhism has developed a variety of means of driving this lesson home, some involving the interpersonal approach that Ram Dass demonstrated for me and some involving meditation practice, which is really practice in restoring the balance between doing and being. One reason for the growing appeal of Buddhism to psychotherapists is because of its success in teaching people how to reconnect with this vital and neglected capacity of the self.

A patient of mine, a successful professional in city government in her early fifties, described her struggles with meditation at her first retreat in terms that clearly reflect this paradigm. While the meditation instructions were simply to *watch* her breath, Kate spent most of the first few days trying hard to *regulate* it. Her breathing should be relaxed, she thought. It should be deep and rhythmical. She should be able to feel every bit of it. Watching the breath became a project, and Kate attacked it with all of the gusto that she regularly applied to difficult problems at work. As she listened to the meditation instructions, however, Kate began to realize that this was not the approach that was being counselled. She saw that her striving led only to a feeling of frustration and failure, but as she tried to change her mode of relating, she began to notice a pain in her abdomen that felt like the constraint of an iron band around her waist. The pain intensified as she approached the end of each exhalation; she began to be aware of a fear as she exhaled, of something like being alone in the vastness of a great desert.

With ample time to explore the ins and outs of this phenomenon, Kate made some breakthroughs. A great caretaker in her intimate relationships, but afraid to let herself be vulnerable, Kate recognized that her approach to the breath was analogous to her approach to her lovers. As long as she could make a project out of them she was fine. But underneath this was a fear that if she was not always doing something, she would be "dropped." If she stayed in control, she did not have to face these fears, but if she were to give it up, she would have to face the horrifying mix of her dependent feelings and her presumptions of her lover's unreliability. She was afraid, she realized, of "falling apart completely."

Kate was comfortable, she began to see, in the realm of manipulation, where doing and being done to are the key modes of relating. But, as the iron band in her abdomen continually reminded her, she was steeling herself against any alternative. Her breath could not be a source of comfort, nor even an object of meditation, unless she first confronted how much she feared annihilation. She needed that iron band to prevent any sudden descent into the abyss.

When we talked all this over after the retreat, Kate smiled ruefully and told me, with some shame, how her mother used to instruct her in her breathing when she was young, teaching her the "right" way to do it. Kate's memory shows that she internalized her mother's inability to let go, which could be seen in her own inability to relax into her breathing in meditation. This need to be in control reflected a basic lack of trust in herself that was very similar to what I had carried into my meeting with Ram Dass.

As my encounter with Ram Dass made clear to me, meditation did not have to be the only venue for Kate's kind of breakthrough. It could also come in the context of a therapeutic relationship in which the need of the ego to maintain control is successfully relinquished. There is nothing about psychotherapy, per se, that could not foster this kind of realization, except that, for many in our culture (both therapists and patients), it is an entirely alien concept. Just as we are taught that doing is preferable to being, so are we reared to think of separateness as the key to our growth and of connection as something that is rooted in childhood.

the transparency of the ego

A linear view of growth and development runs very deeply in our culture, affecting the advice we get about raising our children and the orientation of most of our mental-health professionals. It was articulated most directly by the enormously influential American child psychologist Margaret Mahler in a series of papers written in the 1960s and '70s. The developmental task of the human infant, taught Mahler, is to successfully navigate the path of separation and individuation, two words which under Mahler's influence were gradually merged into a single psychoanalytic mantra: separation/individuation.

Because of Mahler's work, it became generally accepted that the infant is not yet a person. The newborn is merged with the mother, psychologists believed, and development is a sometimes back-and-forth but ultimately unidirectional journey toward greater autonomy and separateness. The human infant is born "prematurely," concluded Mahler, whose descriptions of the stages of development came to permeate all of psychology. The baby is physically separate from the mother but psychologically joined; its task over the first three years of life is, in her famous phrase, one of "hatching."

Only very recently have experts begun to confirm what parents who pay attention have known forever: that the individual is hatched at birth, that there is no state of original union. While the human infant is capable of profound and nourishing oneness with its mother, it is also, already, a separate being, capable of feeling alone. The separations and unions that we experience as adults are present in stripped down and intensified forms in the infant: They characterize life from beginning to end. As Michael Eigen has written in his seminal paper on the topic, "Separateness and connectedness . . . arise together and make each other possible." There is no such thing as "primary fusion" or "undifferentiation"—"Pure merger and isolation are abstract terms which do not characterize living experience."[2]

The belief in original merger has prevented us from appreciating how often we actually drop our ego boundaries in adult life. Whether it is in creative work, in play, while listening to music or playing sports, or in love and sex, the most invigorating aspects of our lives involve the ego's remarkable ability to dissolve itself. Rather than indicating a regression to infantile mental life, these experiences are expressive of a hidden capacity of the psyche that is available to us in all walks of life. When Mahler made separation and individuation into the pinnacle of individual development, she made no allowance for what, in Buddhism, is thought to be the true nature of mind: its ability to shine forth in unrestricted splendor as the self relaxes its boundaries.

Psychology has been suspicious of the wisdom traditions of the world's great religions because these traditions have preserved a capacity of the self that Western psychology has all but whited out. Relegated to the status of a "primitive undifferentiation" that is in fact a fallacy, the melting of the ego has been seen as something that only babies or crazy people do with any regularity. Rather than seeing the self as an expanding and contracting, coalescing and dissolving, separating and merging organism, Western psychology views the self as something that has to be developed or improved throughout its one-way journey toward separateness.

In expounding this view, psychotherapists have deprived us of an essential nutrient, one that the spiritual traditions of the world have struggled to keep alive and that Ram Dass managed to make me glimpse in a single meeting. The ego's permeability is available to us in our daily lives if we can only learn to permit it; the connection that it reveals is the source of a happiness that we yearn for but feel is out of reach. Yet if we continue to see development in linear terms, as proceeding from a merged state of oneness to differentiation and autonomy, we will continue to miss the essential role of letting go in our lives.

In Buddhism, the paradigms are different from separation and individuation. Closer in many ways to the beliefs of contemporary researchers in infancy than to the ideas of nineteenth-century psychoanalysts in its approach to separation and connection, Buddhism rejects the notion of primary fusion in which the infant is merged with the mother. "At birth I was born alone, and at death too I shall die alone," asserted the eighth-century Indian Buddhist scholar and saint Shantideva.[3] The individual is present from the start, asserted Buddha: already separate, playing out and creating her own individual stream of karma (the Sanskrit word for conditioning or cause and effect). When asked once by one of his Western students puzzling over Buddhist teachings of egolessness, "Well then, if there is no self, what is it that reincarnates?" the Tibetan lama Chögyam Trungpa laughed and answered without hesitation.

"Neurosis," he replied.

The Freudian unconscious, which in the Buddhist cosmology of the Wheel of Life is epitomized by core psychological tendencies of greed, hatred, and ignorance, is seen as the driving force of the individual's separateness. But this unconscious mix of blind and self-centered passions and aspirations is not seen as uniquely *un*conscious in Buddhism. It is, in fact, quite often all too conscious.

Separateness, independence, and clear boundaries are not glorified in Buddhism the way they are in our culture. They are seen instead as potent sources of suffering, as illusions that perpetuate destructive emotions like hatred, jealousy, and conceit. As a corollary of this, female attributes are not demonized in Buddhism. Because of the widespread Western belief in the merger of mother and infant, the feminine in our culture cannot escape identification with a dark and overwhelming force that seeks to engulf, swallow, or overcome the masculine properties of separation, reason, and autonomy that Western culture has come to pride itself on. In Buddhism, the feminine principle is not so restricted. It is free to take on another meaning, to assume another role. In the traditional Buddhist images of sexual relations that are used to describe the glory of enlightenment, the male principle embodies the compassionate action of doing while the female connotes primordial wisdom of emptiness, the very ground of being.

This is a very different view of the human personality than the one we grow up with. Rather than seeing ego development as all-important, as Mahler proposed, Buddhism sees the ego as a kind of necessary fiction. We need an ego to function in the world, to carry out tasks, to get us to work on time, to do the laundry, and to master new information. But we have a tendency to overvalue its reality, obscuring a more expansive view of the kinds of connection of which we are capable. In Buddhism, we must surrender the ego so that we can feel our connection to the universe. We do not move toward greater separation and individuation in this view; we move toward love and death.

relaxing the boundaries

There is a bar in my neighborhood that is known for its unique bathrooms that serves as a good metaphor for this alternative view of the ego. The bathrooms have a special quality that people speak about in almost reverential tones. They are up a flight of stairs and seem to have the second story all to themselves. They are large and modern, made of steel, chrome, glass, and European porcelain. But their distinguishing characteristics are their doors, which are made entirely of glass and are transparent. Only when people go into the bathroom and close the door behind them does the glass become opaque, shielding them from the eyes of the waiting crowd. When they emerge and the door closes again behind them, it regains its previous transparency. Over and over again, people watch the door cloud over and then clear itself, delighted at its capacity to tease and at the same time hoping for a momentary breakdown in its action.

These doors strike me as the perfect metaphor for the ego: It comes into being when we have to go to the bathroom but is otherwise invisible. It has no ongoing, intrinsic reality. Poised between inner and outer, the ego is like a membrane. When it becomes permeable, our boundaries are temporarily lifted. When we prevent this permeability and instead inflate the ego's "reality," we are in effect erecting impermeable walls and creating our own isolation. When we learn to leave the ego alone, however, we discover that it does not have any ongoing durability. Released from our self-imposed walling off, we find ourselves connecting more deeply with whatever surrounds us.

As an example of this, a patient of mine, a photographer

named Maya came to me complaining of a recurrent and disturbing dream of an intruder breaking into her house. Thinking first in a classical mode, I wondered to myself what feeling or urge she was afraid of, what aspect of her unconscious this intruder might represent. But something made me wait before floating such an idea.

While it did contain this motif, Maya's dream was suggestive of something more. Maya felt that she had to be capable at all times, that nothing could ever be out of control in her life. Whenever this control was challenged—by her child's chicken pox, the disarray of her home renovation, her husband's moods, or her own negative feelings—she became despondent. In her dream, whenever the intruder broke in, Maya would become powerless to speak or to act. Mindful of how identified Maya was with her coping abilities, with her separated and individuated self, I suggested to her that perhaps, as Freud originally proposed, her dream was actually a wish. Perhaps she was secretly looking for a way to break a hole in her armor of capacity. Perhaps standing there powerless was exactly what she was seeking, although she did not know how to do it.

Maya's difficulty, I thought, lay in an insufficient development of her capacity to be. It was not that her unconscious was so threatening that it had to be tamed further, but that she had not learned how to ride the waves of that which she could not control. She was an expert at coping but uncomfortable with silence, overly reliant on her ability to figure everything out. Very early in her life Maya had lost touch with her ability to put herself on pause. She had grown up fast but on a very insecure foundation. Imprisoned by the very qualities that she had built up so strongly, she had sought therapy with the unstated hope that I could help make the first chink in her armor.

Just as separation and connectedness make each other possible, so do the male and female elements of doing and being. One is not "primary," nor is one always preferable, yet we are deficient if we cannot go freely from one mode into the other. This is what Maya needed to learn. She needed to recover a trust in her own capacity to let go.

One of the powerful consequences of my introductory experiences with the spiritual traditions of the East was that I became much less afraid of being with another person without being in control of the situation, a useful capacity in my role as a psychotherapist. And meditation further encouraged a trust that was difficult for me to find elsewhere, a trust in surrendering to the moment, to an emotional experience, no matter how threatening. Yet what I subsequently found was that I tended to get in the way of that trust by clinging to my newfound ability as if it would vanish without constant reinforcement. As Buddhism reminds us, we can cling to anything, even letting go. It took a much later therapeutic encounter to point this out to me.

A number of years after my initial exposure to meditation, when I was approaching my midthirties, I began a course of therapy and supervision with a senior Gestalt therapist in New York City, a man named Isadore From. I was already a therapist by this time, and Isadore was renowned as a teacher of therapists. He was a lovely man but exquisitely sensitive to any note of artifice. If I were to say to him, for instance, "I *really* like her!" he would immediately ask me what I did *not* like about the person in question. My use of "really" would strike him as an exaggeration that hid an ulterior meaning, and he would usually be right. He was a difficult man to hide from. In one of my first meetings with him, after completing a particular exchange, I reflexively prolonged my gaze, attempting to preserve and extend the eye contact that we had established. This was a strategy that, in retrospect, I believe I had cultivated since my encounter with Ram Dass, meaning to convey a sense of openness and availability, spiced with a dash of meaningfulness.

"Are you aware that you are staring at me?" Isadore asked after a moment. "Blink!"

Once again, my fragile relationship to the capacity for being was revealed. I had turned it into something that I *did* instead of letting it be something that I *was*. Made anxious by the impending loss of connection, I was attempting to forestall the inevitable return to my own separateness by artificially prolonging my eye contact. It was like refusing to stop eating ice cream, not wanting to give up the taste, even though I was already full.

As Isadore made me see, my anxiety about losing that state introduced an artificial note into something that in its very nature is natural, spontaneous, and fleeting. Connection may be our natural state, as Buddhism teaches, but it is not static. Part of trusting in it is to let our experience of it come and go. While I was much more comfortable with my own capacity for silent communication, I still did not really trust that the connection I so valued was infinite and renewable. While he would never define himself as "spiritual" (having the same disdain for that word as he did for "really"), Isadore taught me a very subtle, but essential, spiritual lesson. To experience true connection I had to be willing to come back into myself.

This is a common frustration at the beginning of spiritual work. Once we discover that it is possible to relax the ego's grip, we try to package this ability so that it will be there to prop us up. But this attempt at mastery immediately distances us from our goal—it introduces a note of falseness into something that happens naturally if left alone. The moment of first eye contact need not become a lifeless stare, as it did in my interaction with Isadore. If real, and therefore mutual, it makes us smile instead.

part three

EMBRACING

releasing your heart

The antidote to hatred in the heart, the source of violence, is tolerance. Tolerance is an important virtue of bodhisattvas (enlightened heroes and heroines)—it enables you to refrain from reacting angrily to the harm inflicted on you by others. You could call this practice "inner disarmament," in that a well-developed tolerance makes you free from the compulsion to counterattack. For the same reason, we also call tolerance the "best armor," since it protects you from being conquered by hatred itself.

THE DALAI LAMA

5
tolerance

When Freud gave his instructions to physicians practicing psychoanalysis, he compared the process to the newly invented telephone. Turn your unconscious toward that of the patient as one telephone receiver is attuned to another, he suggested. Only then can the vibrations that underlie the verbal communications be felt. As this process was clarified, it became clear that feeling states in particular pass across human boundaries with remarkable ease. Therapists first described this in people whose anger was so personally unacceptable that they seemed to be completely unaware of it. When sitting with such patients, the therapist would often find herself filled with an inexplicable rage that had to be decoded and reintroduced to the patient in order for there to be any progress in the therapy. Yet this process, which came to be called projective identification, is not limited to fury, nor is it always pathological. Sometimes it is simply necessary.

When my son was in kindergarten, about midway through the school year, he suddenly became extremely clingy whenever we dropped him off anywhere. At school, at gymnastics, at a friend's house, at a birthday party: he became tearful and anxious at times that had previously not been at all difficult for him. At first we ignored the problem, hoping that it would disappear by itself. Then we tried to figure it out, which led to all kinds of theories but no improvement. Then we tried a confusing mix of talking to him, bribing him with Pez candy, and staying close to him at all times. Nothing worked.

Finally a friend of mine, a child analyst named Robbie Stein, was over for lunch and we discussed the problem (at my wife's insistence). He suggested that we set aside a half hour every night to play with a specially chosen set of toys with our son. Nothing could interrupt us and we should just let the play take over. Ready to try anything, my wife gathered a number of assorted figures and objects and put them in a shoebox that we set in a special place and called "the box." My son took to it at once, and thus we added a new element to our nightly bedtime ritual.

On the third night, my son and I were playing that two characters were having a playdate, and he kept saying, "Come on, my daddy will make you dinner, my daddy will make you pizza." Proud as I am of my contribution to the home environment, I knew this scenario to be unusual.

"Your daddy?" I said, rousing myself from a rather inattentive and languorous state. "What about your mommy?"

"Oh," he said matter-of-factly, "she's dead. Or she's not really dead, her mother's dead. What's that thing you die of, Daddy?"

"Cancer," I said, slowly putting two and two together.

Several months earlier my mother-in-law had been diagnosed with uterine cancer, had been hospitalized for surgery, and was now receiving radiation treatments. We thought we had shielded the kids from all of this, but we were wrong. My son's anxiety over death had turned a matter-of-fact good-bye embrace into a nightmare of clinging, and we retrieved this information only by letting him be in bits and pieces in his play.

As we sat there among the play figures, I was able to reassure him on a couple of different levels. Some people do die from cancer, I explained, but not everyone. Grandma was being treated, just like Grandpa had been, and she wasn't feeling sick anymore. We all thought she was going to live until she was very old. I read to him a children's book about an elderly Tibetan woodcarver who gets old and dies. I could feel my son grappling with the reality of not just Grandma's death but of his and ours. Yet the feeling was not morose or depressing. He had his excitement and his energy back; he was completely engaged in his own inimitable and electric way. With the topic out in the open, he began to relax. After a short time he had had enough. The door to his room burst open and he was off. Death had entered into our vocabulary, and my son put an end to his clinging at routine separations.

the capacity to feel

This interaction with my son reminded me of some of the most surprising encounters of my early years as a therapist with hospitalized patients. It was not unusual for me to find myself sitting alone with a newly admitted patient who seemed in total crisis, embroiled in intense feelings over which she seemed to have little control. These young men or women (for they were usually young) would be filled with rage or sadness or fear, but upon getting to know them, I would discover that they were remarkably unaware of what they were feeling. They could act their feelings out, but they did not seem to know what they were. They were by no means crazy, in the conventional sense of the word, but they seemed to have no idea of what was happening to them, of why they were starving themselves or cutting themselves or threatening suicide if left alone by their boyfriends or girlfriends.

As I got to know these people even better, I began to see that not only did they not know what they were feeling, but they had remarkably little idea of what feelings even were.

They had no vocabulary for their emotions. Reacting with fear every time certain physical or emotional sensations became prominent, it was as if they were phobic toward their own feelings. Only when they went back to the beginning and learned the basics of what emotions actually are—what we call "mad, sad, and glad"—could they develop the capacity to tolerate feelings.

Psychoanalysis has some very interesting things to say about the origins of emotional experience and about how people end up in the situation of these patients. Especially in early life, feelings are generally not understood until they are taken up by another person and given back in more palatable form. A baby who is uncomfortable because her diaper needs changing does not think to herself, "I'm mad because Mommy isn't paying attention." She simply feels unpleasant physical sensations and then mounting internal frustration. When her mother notices what is going on and then interprets for her ("There, there, it's okay, don't be so mad. I'm here. Let's get you changed."), the baby gradually learns that those mounting internal feelings are called "mad." Her mother contains the baby's feelings and translates them back to her in a more digestible form.

In addition, a parent is faced early in a child's life with the full intensity of the child's ruthless pursuit of her own needs. Children have a single-minded and aggressive desire for contact that can often feel overwhelming to a parent who is expecting sweetness and light. A parent's duty, in the face of this emotional assault, is not to withdraw or to retaliate. It is to survive. This survival sends a message to a young child that her emotions are not scary or destructive.[1]

I remember an exchange with my daughter when she was in kindergarten that confirmed this point for me. We had had a fight that morning that had escalated, and I had given her a "time-out," requiring her to sit quietly for a minute by herself. A bit worried about how she had reacted to this, I walked her to school afterward and stood by in the playground as she went rushing up to several of her friends. Immediately, her conversation turned to the morning's exchange.

"Do you know what my daddy does when I'm bad?" she asked her friends excitedly. "He gives me a time-out!"

I understood at once that my daughter was proud of my ability to withstand her feelings. She had not felt my reaction to be a retaliation, nor had she absorbed a message that she was dangerous. I had been able to contain her feelings, and she was not left with a sense that she had to repair anything in her relationship with me.

All of our intimate relationships, not just parent-child ones, have intense emotional exchanges that test our ability to know and bear feelings. When I first fell in love, in my adult years, I travelled with my future wife to a rocky point on the coast of Maine that had always been special to me. As I embraced her, with the surf pounding around us, we were both filled with a sense not just of love but of death, as if we were holding on tightly to each other while our lives passed before us, or as if we were mourning a dead child. We did not know where these feelings came from nor why we were both having them, but they seemed to have something to do with an implicit sense of the preciousness of our love. Just as my son needed us to take in his dread of death and make it make sense, so were we spontaneously making sense out of each other's most intimate emotions.

As Freud discovered in his writings about the countryside, beauty carries with it the seed of mourning over its eventual demise. In our hug on the beach we were breathing each other's emotions, making them make sense in a way we could only do with each other's help. Lovers often inject breath into each other's emotions, as parents do in a different way with their children, making those very feelings more tolerable by virtue of their being exchanged and known.

In a quite similar way, it is not uncommon for me to be sitting with a relatively new patient, listening to the details of a particular problem, and to suddenly feel, out of the blue, a sudden fear or sadness that always takes me by surprise. It is as if an unanticipated visitor has suddenly arrived and I am unsure of whose friend she is. "Who invited you?" I want to say. The more conventional approach to understanding this phenomenon is to assume that something in what the patient is saying is triggering an emotional response in me based on my own past, on my own unconscious material. But this is not the only possibility. There are times when the feeling proves to have come from the patient.

Both the ancient tradition of Buddhist psychology and the modern one of psychotherapy recognize that recovering the capacity to feel is crucial to their disciplines. There can be no wholeness without an integration of feelings. The paradox that both traditions have discovered is that, while we seek to integrate feelings, the only way to access them is through a state of unintegration. We need a state of reverie to know our emotions. This reverie both gives us space, as Winnicott described, and allows us to take in others' feelings, as therapists have discovered. As the psychologist and writer Gregory Bateson used to say, "It takes two to know one."[2]

Rather than learning how to be tolerant of difficult feelings, many of us have learned only to avoid them. As with my hospitalized patients, our inclination is often to run from our emotions because they carry with them the threat of destruction. Indulging ourselves in thinking as a protective alternative, we try to avoid our fear by staying aloof of our feelings.

taming the heart

In an ancient Buddhist sutra called the *Anguttara Nikaya* the Buddha extolled the value of what he called the "tamed heart," while warning against the dangers of not being touched in this way. "I know nothing which is as intractable as an untamed

heart, . . ." he declared. "I know nothing which brings suffering as does an untamed, uncontrolled, unattended, and un-
restrained heart. . . . I know nothing which brings joy as
does a tamed, controlled, attended, and restrained heart.[3]

For a child, the taming of the heart occurs when a parent
survives the onslaught of the child's emotions. In psychotherapy, the prototype for the taming of the heart is the reciprocal
exchange of feelings like that which occurred when we played
"the box" with my son. In meditation, the taming of the heart
takes place through the gradual cultivation of mindfulness, in
which nonjudgmental awareness is extended from the body to
feelings, emotions, and states of mind. In its interpersonal
method, psychotherapy has created a unique situation in
which the flow of feelings between people can be tapped and
acknowledged. In its cultivation of awareness, meditation seeks
to create an inner holding environment in which the raw material of emotional experience can be reintroduced and made
use of. While the methods may differ, the intent is the same:
to recover a capacity for feelings that we are all somewhat
afraid of.

Many of us come to psychotherapy or meditation or other
avenues of personal transformation because our lives are restricted by our own unacknowledged feelings. We carry with
us a feeling of falseness, or an excessive intellectuality, that
wraps around and obscures our hidden emotional capacity. I
was given a good example of this in my work when a univer-

sity professor named Olivia managed to evoke in me an intense feeling of frustration, despite being one of the kindest and most intelligent people I had ever treated. Olivia did not know that she was making me feel frustrated, and it took me a while to figure out that this frustration I was feeling actually belonged to Olivia.

In session after session I would feel myself reaching to understand what she was saying and falling just short. She would describe power struggles at work with just enough vagueness that I would never be quite sure of who was who or of where the difficulty lay. When I would try to clarify the picture by asking questions, her answers would lead me further astray. She told me ornate dreams that involved labyrinthine passageways with endless numbers of doorways, vistas, and characters such that I could never be sure where to focus. We had wonderful intellectual discussions that served as a kind of reassurance to us both that we could understand each other, but time and again I would return to a feeling of frustrated confusion coupled with a recurrent wish that I could be of more help to her.

Finally I had enough sense to focus both of our attention on the feeling of frustration that I was experiencing. Our attention to this frustration elicited a series of associations for Olivia that culminated in a story of how she had been hospitalized with a life-threatening infection when six months old and kept in isolation for a month. This was a story that Olivia had been told, but it was not one that she had ever actually remembered. Her hands and arms had been wrapped and padded, Olivia told me, to prevent her from chafing the skin off of them as she thrashed about her bed in frustration. For weeks on end, Olivia had been kept in a sterile chamber in the hospital. Her frustration from that time seemed to still be alive in her.

By being so vague in our sessions, Olivia was managing to re-create this un-worked-through frustration in me. It was as if it were too dangerous for her to experience it all by herself. As she began to take it back from me—to connect up the feeling with the story—Olivia became much less vague in her sessions. She also became more able to tolerate frustration whenever she was left in the lurch by her coworkers or was not supported adequately by her boss. These situations lost some of their mysterious force once she understood how vulnerable she was to any kind of frustrating circumstances. Rather than just acting her feelings out, as my son was doing in his clinging and as Olivia was doing in her vagueness, she actually learned how to feel them.

four foundations of mindfulness

In his description of the "Four Foundations of Mindfulness," the Buddha taught the method by which we can reestablish rapport with ourselves. In certain ways, his approach is very similar to that which occurs in psychotherapy as well, but he was able to outline it in an almost cookbook-like manner. First and foremost comes mindfulness of the body, in which the direct physical sensations of breathing and bodily experience are made the objects of meditation. When I first began to practice meditation intensively, I found that my sense of myself *in my body* was dramatically increased. This is the foundation of any successful meditation practice and the source of much of its power. As I also discovered, this can be as frustrating as it is rewarding because of the mind's inevitable tendency to pull itself away from the body. Mindfulness of the body is a lesson in how much time we spend in obsessive and repetitive thought. One of my patients, back from his first ten-day silent retreat, described it as "circling endlessly in the eddies of my mind."

Buddhism offers a rather paradoxical message about all of this. While asserting, over and over again, that "all is *mind*," Buddhist teachers also emphasize the defensive, or avoidant, nature of much of our thinking activity. "If we are not our thoughts," I have often questioned, "then what are we?" In emphasizing the importance of *mind*, Buddhism is clearly pointing to something other than the brain or the thinking apparatus. *Mind* is not localized in the head in Buddhism; indeed, the same word is often used interchangeably for mind and heart. Healing, in Buddhism, means opening up a connection to this mind through the practice of meditation.

One of my patients, a mother of three young children, had

a sincere interest in learning about such meditation but absolutely no free time to meditate. Like many parents, Abbie felt obligated to her family but oppressed by their constant demands and frustrated by her inability to make time for herself. I explained to her that meditation need not be done exclusively in a silent environment or in a cross-legged position, that the Buddha had taught meditation in four postures: sitting, lying down, walking, and standing. The idea was to develop awareness of bodily experience or, at first, to develop awareness of how little awareness there was of bodily experience.

Abbie decided, after some experimentation, that she could use her time in the kitchen to practice. "As long as I'm in the kitchen, everyone leaves me alone," she laughed. Standing at the sink washing dishes, Abbie began to consciously focus on her posture, on how she held her body, and on how she shifted her weight. She was incredulous of how much tension she had. She found that she was holding her body in all kinds of unnatural positions which only served to exacerbate the feelings of strain that she was struggling against.

Abbie felt chagrined by this discovery and as if this too was a sign of how messed up she was, but I congratulated her for her accomplishment in meditation. She had discovered the chronic state in which most of us spend most of our time. Lost in thought, cut off from our bodies, nursing a grievance or two, with physical and emotional tension accumulating outside of awareness, we perpetuate the very sense of frustration that we struggle against. Mindfulness of the body opens this up so that we can begin the process of getting to know ourselves.

Contact with the body develops the ability to be with feelings. The physical tension that Abbie discovered was the perfect vehicle for the exploration of her psyche. Rather than walling herself off from difficult feelings, she learned to literally breathe in and out of her anxiety-ridden states, using her body as the forum to learn about her feelings.

Mindfulness of feelings, which involves meditation on the pleasant and unpleasant aspects of bodily experience, is the next foundation of mindfulness. Since feeling states are experienced primarily in the body, the ability to maintain a continuous state of physical awareness gives an enormous boost to the capacity to bear feelings. This is fortunate because one of the most common occurrences in beginning meditation involves the reexperiencing of terrifying feelings. These are the core states that were often impossible to process in childhood because of parental absence or interference. Even in meditation, these feelings can still seem intolerable, but the entire thrust of meditation practice is designed to increase their tolerability. This can be a frightening experience, as many of my patients have discovered.

Because mindfulness of feelings involves the careful attention to the flow of pleasant and unpleasant sensation in the body, there is none of the usual picking and choosing that otherwise colors our experience. When I was instructed in this method, I was taught to simply note whatever I was feeling: pleasant, unpleasant, or neutral. My observing mind functioned almost as another person, watching the flow of sensation with relative ease. This created a very different relationship with my internal world than the one I was used to. My chronic tendency was to shrink from the unpleasant and reach for the pleasant. Mindfulness of feelings encouraged a dispassionate acceptance of both.

This becomes very interesting as meditation progresses because, as we pay more attention to our bodily experience, we inevitably come upon those early traumas that we have shied away from. It seems as if they are stored in our bodies, waiting for us to stumble upon them. A patient of mine named Dale, for example, came back from an intensive meditation retreat and described how a pain in her neck had become the principal focus of her nine-day retreat. As she tried to experience the flow of unpleasant sensations emanating from this pain, she became intolerably anxious. Her mind produced waves of catastrophic imagery. For many days she took this anxiety to be some kind of failure on her part rather than trusting that it was part of her process of unfolding.

Only when she learned to apply mindfulness of feelings to her cascades of worry and anxious thought did she discover the true power of her meditation. By not backing away from those unpleasant feelings, she was able to see how anxiety had colored her experience since early childhood and how scared she was by it. Seeing her anxiety as a sign of failure was not a new reaction for Dale; it was one that she had had for as long as she could remember. Once she was reassured that her up-surge of anxiety did not disqualify her as a meditator, she was able to continue with her practice, discovering, for the first time in her life, that she was able to bear more anxiety than she had thought. As her fears settled down, Dale was able to relax around her pain and, as is often the case, the unpleasant sensa-tions in her neck began to ease.

mind weeds

In just this way, mindfulness of feelings merges into mindful-ness of thoughts and emotions, the third of the four founda-tions of mindfulness. Beginning with the body, extending first to feelings and then to more complex states of mind, mindful-ness allows us to explore those aspects of our experience, like our day-to-day thoughts, that we usually take for granted. As Dale discovered, once we are able to breathe in and out of difficult feeling states, we observe how much of our routine thinking is rooted in avoidance of these very emotions. This is precisely what those psychotherapists in the tradition of D. W. Winnicott have discovered in treating people who complain of feeling estranged from life.

When children's emotional states are not accepted by their parents, the children's own thinking has to step in and try to manage the situation. Unable to process feelings by themselves, such children begin talking to themselves, trying to protect against the onslaught of their own emotional states. It was easy to imagine Dale as an anxious child, for instance, with parents who were too frightened of anxiety themselves to help her with her own. Much of the endless circling of thought that we discover in meditation seems to serve this compensatory and protective function.

The most basic fear experienced by people coming to see me for therapy is of being overwhelmed by the force of their own emotions if they relax the grip of their egos. They fear that if they give up control, they will lose control, that their unconscious will, if given a chance, rise up and inundate them. In some way, this reflects the classic view of the unconscious as a seething cauldron of demonic forces that have to be tamed by the light of reason and analysis. While respecting the power and complexity of the Freudian unconscious, my Buddhist understanding has made me suspicious of my patients' fears. It is my experience that emotions, no matter how powerful, are not overwhelming if given room to breathe. Contained within the vastness of awareness, our emotions have the power to connect us with each other rather than driving us apart. Mindfulness can serve as a vehicle for desensitizing ourselves to our fears of our own feelings, breaking down the self-imposed barriers that keep us at a distance, not just from each other, but from ourselves.

When one of the first Japanese Zen masters to teach in the West, Suzuki Roshi of the San Francisco Zen Center, taught his students how to pay attention to their thoughts, he instructed them to trace them back to their roots. "Thoughts are like weeds," he stressed, and they can be pulled up by their roots and used to fertilize the garden of mind. I think Suzuki Roshi was pointing to just this compensatory activity of thought in his instructions. If we can establish a rapport with the emotional experience that takes place primarily in our bodies, we do not need to think so much. Thought is not the enemy in meditation as so many people would like to believe. Thinking is quite useful when there is something to ponder. But defensive thinking just makes us feel cut off.

Thinking quiets down in meditation because the excessive mental activity is no longer necessary once these connections are made. When emotional states are experienced in their entirety, rather than as fleeting shadows in the recesses of the mind, thinking is not quite so important. In tracing thoughts back to their roots, back to the original feeling states, we get out of our heads and return to our senses. A different experience of mind is then possible, one that the Buddha points to in his fourth foundation of mindfulness.

After we have established a rapport with the body, with feelings, and with mental and emotional states, the Buddha suggested that we could have a new relationship with our minds. This is the fourth foundation: mindfulness of mind. In speaking of *mind* the Buddha was not referring to thought, or even to the thinker of thoughts. He was referring to something closer to the Western notion of psyche.[4] Psyche is more like the container in which thoughts and feelings happen. It is like the underlying nervous system that connects the mind-body process. In Buddhism it is compared to clear space—the big blue sky of mind.

In healthy development, it seems, the mind does not have to take over prematurely and organize a person's experience; the environment (in the form of parental activity) can be trusted to do this. This frees the mind up for another activity, which the child analyst D. W. Winnicott delicately described as *understanding*. No parent can be perfect, he pointed out, but they need only be good enough. When they *are* good enough, the child learns to make use of the parents' "relative failure" rather than compensating for an absolute failure with excessive mental activity. In "making use of" their parents' failures, children germinate the capacity for empathy. The function of the mind, implied Winnicott, is not thinking. It is tolerance.[5]

the release from perfection

When a child is raised in a holding environment that is good enough, that child's mind gradually takes on the character of her parent's acceptance. When difficult feelings arise, the child trusts that they can be filtered through the parent or borne in the psyche in the interim. When the parents inevitably fail to be present at a time of need, the mind develops the capacity to not take their failure personally and to be tolerant of their absence. "What releases the mother from her need to be near-perfect is the infant's understanding,[6] said Winnicott. The child gradually develops the knowledge of her parents as separate beings and is not catastrophically threatened by their separateness. We do not really *need* perfection, implied Winnicott, we only need a mind that is capable of generosity.

For most of us, this optimal path of development does not proceed so smoothly. Rather than minds of tolerance, we are more likely to have minds of judgment that we experience as beyond our voluntary control. Much of the time, our minds seem to have minds of their own. When the Buddha gave his original teachings on meditation, he did so in a way that was meant to counter this condition. He laid out a process designed to heal the split that we feel from our own minds. The four foundations of mindfulness permit the mind to take on its inherent capacity for tolerance.

I had an experience on a recent meditation retreat that illuminated much of this for me. I had been looking forward to the retreat, eight days away from all of my responsibilities as a parent and a therapist, and to being in the country, free to take long walks and explore the outdoors. I arrived at the meditation center in the late evening, began my retreat with a brief meditation before bed, and awoke in the early morning with chills and a scratchy throat. It was pouring outside and windy and cold, and despite my firmest intent, I was unable to go outside without feeling absolutely awful.

In addition to my struggle with the flu, a number of other minor inconveniences, such as the quality of the food and the banging of the heating pipes at night, began to bother me. The weather eventually cleared up, but as it turns out, it was hunting season and the still country air was routinely punctuated by shotgun blasts. Long walks in the woods suddenly seemed much less attractive. Through all of this, I engaged myself in my meditation practice, dutifully noting my reactions and returning to my breathing and bodily experience. I took Tylenol and naps and sat through much of my illness.

My mind became quite still, but I had the uncomfortable sense of hanging back just a bit, of being at a slight remove from all that was happening within and around me. After about five days I had my first interview with Joseph Goldstein, my teacher at the retreat. I described my sense of remove to him and gradually admitted to all of the little dissatisfactions that I was struggling with. My cold, the rain, the food, my inability to exercise—one by one I confessed to how, underneath my stillness of mind, I was still unhappy with the general tenor of things.

"Oh, I've spent a lot of time in that place," said Joseph. "It's not the way you wanted it to be, is it?"

I felt silly to be falling into such an obvious trap of letting my expectations interfere with what was actually happening, but I also felt an all-too-familiar sadness creeping up from my chest to my eyes. In the stillness of the retreat I saw how I did this a lot: envisioning how something, or someone, had to be perfect, and then being disappointed when they failed, pulling myself back into a sullen remove. Here I was doing it again.

"You know what I sometimes do?" said Joseph, referring in particular to my cold and discomfort. "I pretend that I'm dying and that there's nothing to be done. Rather than judging it, take no position in your mind. Stop leaning into circumstances," he continued, "and rest in your own awareness."

Joseph's words resonated and helped me immeasurably in my retreat. Unknowingly, he was paraphrasing Winnicott's observation that the infant's understanding releases the mother from perfection. Only by developing the ability of my mind to take no position could I begin to do that. In recovering my sadness at the impossibility of my demands, but in not treating that sadness as special, I was learning a lesson that Buddhism teaches over and over again: Uncovering difficult feelings does not make them go away but does enable us to practice tolerance and understanding with the entirety of our being. As Joseph made clear, it is not just the mother that has to be released from perfection. It is everything.

6
relationship

When the Buddha achieved his enlightenment, it was after a week of sitting in continuous meditation, wrestling with his own demons. Immediately after his breakthrough he reached down with one hand to touch the earth, a pose that is reproduced in Buddhist sculptures all over Asia. The traditional stories suggest that the Buddha was calling the earth as witness to his enlightenment, but there is more to the posture than that. The Buddha, by his gesture, was suggesting that he had touched, and been touched by, the root of his being. He had passed through all illusions of identity and reached the far shore of pure awareness. But in touching the earth the Buddha was indicating something even more. He was demonstrating that the ground of his being was his interconnection with the world.

In order to reach this understanding, the Buddha had to find a way through himself. He had to leave all of his relationships and go deeply inside himself to confront his own separateness. In the Four Noble Truths, his first oral teachings after his enlightenment, the Buddha attempted to spell out what he had found. The more we come to terms with our own separateness, taught the Buddha, the more we can feel the connections that are already there. The Buddha had to leave his relationships in order to discover his capacity to relate. Explicitly using the metaphor of a path, he described the Eightfold Path as the key to uncovering this capacity.

In the centuries since this first teaching, it has become customary to speak of the spiritual path as if it were something like a well-marked highway with entrance ramps and speed limits and even rest stops or service stations. People speak of being "on the path" as if it were clear where it starts and stops. But if we look at what the Buddha actually taught, we see immediately that his Eightfold Path of Right Livelihood—Action, Speech, Mindfulness, Concentration, Effort, Understanding, and Thought—are really parameters rather than way stations on a journey. The spiritual path means *making* a path rather than following one. It is a very personal process, unique to each individual.

I was reminded of this not long ago when on vacation in

Maine. My family shares a small piece of oceanfront property with a number of other families, and we had to have a path built through a common lot so that everyone could have access to the ocean. After much debate, some local contractors were engaged to build a path from the common driveway down a sloping and thickly wooded patch of stream- and root-filled forest to the beach. One option was to bulldoze a straight path from start to finish using heavy machinery, and the other was to respect the contours of the forest and to wind a path around boulders and large trees while gradually working toward the shore. This latter process, which mercifully was the chosen option, produced a lovely and varied, twisting and turning, delightful path through the forest. But it was a lot of work for the contractors who had to pick their way with relatively small tools through the unforgiving forest.

This work struck me as a perfect metaphor for the kind of path the Buddha had in mind. In building a path through the self to the far shore of awareness, we have to carefully pick our way through our own wilderness. If we can put our minds into a place of surrender, we will have an easier time feeling the contours of the land. We do not have to break our way through as much as we have to find our way around the major obstacles. We do not have to cure every neurosis, we just have to learn how not to be caught by them.

This is a difficult process because of how restricted our capacities for attention usually are. We do not suspend our judgments easily, nor do we generally have access to our childhood capacity for curiosity and exploration. Our attentional resources are hijacked early in our lives by our need to manage the intrusive or ignoring familial environments in which we are immersed. As a result, many of us end up in unreal states, stuck in our heads, unaware of our bodies, and unaware of being unaware.

In making a path like the Buddha, we discover our own capacities for relationship. Doing this is like feeling our way in the dark. We need a healthy appreciation for what kind of obstacles we are facing within ourselves, and we need a method for working our way around those obstacles. It is in this sense that the path is the goal—opening leads to further opening. The Buddha's meditative teachings are about finding and incorporating a method around our obstacles. They are as relevant in today's world of psychotherapy as they were when the Buddha first reached down and touched the earth.

meditation in action

When I first entered psychotherapy, some years into my embrace of Buddhism, it was still with a sense of wanting to break out of myself in some way. After my experience with Ram Dass and my immersion in meditation, I had decided to enter medical school as a prelude to becoming a psychiatrist. The more familiar I became with meditation, the more I was aware that progress on the spiritual path meant a willingness to explore my emotional life as the Buddha had indicated in his teachings on the Four Foundations of Mindfulness. Opening my attention to body, feelings, emotions, and mind did not have to be restricted to the meditation cushion. It was a process I could attempt in all aspects of my life and was certainly one I could pursue with a therapist. Despite my earlier unsatisfactory experience with therapy, I became interested in giving it another try.

Guided to a Gestalt therapist named Michael Vincent Miller by my housemate Francis (who was himself a meditator studying Gestalt therapy), I remember being asked in my first session what I wanted to get out of therapy. It was a simple question, but it shook me up. I had just arrived, after all. Wasn't it enough that I was there? Couldn't I just surrender and let therapy do its thing? Wasn't he supposed to help me plumb the depths of my unconscious to find out what I was truly after? I did not really know what I wanted, but I was being asked by this somewhat mercurial man to take responsibility for wanting something. Wasn't this awfully *personal?*

I was intrigued enough by my predicament to not flee precipitously. I must have known on some level that what I wanted was to be able to say what I wanted. I fumbled around for a while and said something about wishing that I could be more spontaneous, or more original, or more dynamic in my expression of myself. Michael nodded sympathetically, at which I took offense. He then asked me if I was aware that I was sitting on the edge of my seat.

I was not aware of it. I was sitting the way I always sat when talking with someone. What was wrong with the way I was sitting, I wanted to ask. But I remained silent, feeling suddenly trapped and at the same time noticing a flicker of glee deep inside me. This man was going to help me: I could feel it.

Michael waited, as if to give me time to get over my sudden self-consciousness and to actually notice how I was sitting. He was right. I was perched like a bird on the edge of my chair. I was very uncomfortable there. "You give yourself no support," he said softly.

I spent the rest of the session feeling what it was like to sit back in my chair, making use of my whole body as I spoke. It required a good deal of effort to not just float back up into my head, but I could feel already that I was forging a connection with the physical environment that I had been denying myself. My body *was* the unconscious that I was so interested in plumbing. For all of my meditation training, I still needed the help of a therapist to show me where I was holding back.

"Form is emptiness," the Buddhists teach, but form is also form. I would never be able to approach the emptiness of form if I continued to deny myself the experience of it.

In my own way, I was dramatizing the scenario that Winnicott described so beautifully in his articles on excessive thinking. Distanced from my own body and lodged somewhere in my thinking mind, I was as estranged from my own creative abilities as I was removed from the support of my chair. There was a connection between inhabiting my body and opening up a creative mental space from which I could use words to articulate myself.

My therapist could just as easily have been a Zen master in the manner in which he related to me, only he was not. For me, his teaching did not in any way contradict what I had already put together for myself from my years of practicing meditation; it merely drove home the lesson on another front, in a particularly vivid and helpful way. The lesson about being more in my body was not particularly new, but it was presented to me in a new way. We do not get lots of realizations in our lives as much as we get the same ones over and over.

There was something about this therapy that was very different from what I had expected, and that has influenced me tremendously in my own work. Michael did not present himself as an authority figure who "analyzed" my psychic configurations. He did not interpret my Oedipal dilemma, at least not in so many words. He was not remote and silent. He was very available, quite humorous and playful, and he was always wondering where I was. He paid particular attention to what prevented me from being part of the relationship with him.

Intuitively, I recognized that his ongoing question, of where was I, was my own question as well. It had driven my interest in meditation and had propelled me into therapy. Through the power of therapy I started to see that I was most identified with who I was when I was anxious, yet I felt most myself when I could relate unself-consciously. This presented me with a bit of a paradox. Throughout the course of this therapy I would always arrive at a rather intimidating conclusion: The only way to find out where I was was to get out of the way and let myself happen.

This makes the process sound too passive, however. Getting out of the way was essential: Dislodging myself from my over-indulgence in my thinking mind was a necessary precursor to any kind of satisfying encounter. But letting myself happen was not quite the voyeuristic process that it sounds. My therapist was asking something of me that was more on the order of improvisation. He was asking for meditation *in action*, not for a mere witnessing of psychic debris.

playing

When I first discovered Buddhism I found that it authenticated a feeling of emptiness that I had long harbored. I had never felt as real as I thought I was supposed to feel, but with the wisdom of Buddhism behind me I stopped trying to feel more real than I did. My initial experiences in meditation taught me a receptive kind of surrender that gave me a sense of deepening, opening, and acceptance. This gave me back a tremendous freedom—the freedom to just be how I was. My therapy with Michael Vincent Miller worked in harmony with this discovery. Just as the Buddha taught that we should begin with mindfulness of the body, so did Michael direct my attention there. Just as the Buddha taught that giving up our premature notions of who or what we are leads to a more authentic feeling of self, so did Michael encourage me to improvise without being tripped up by my own self-consciousness. I came to see that this was an active aspect of surrender. Rather than opening into the unknown, this was more of a letting go into spontaneity and self-expression.

My most vivid memory of this period of therapy is of a time when I was completely unsure of what to talk about and anxiously casting about for a topic when I caught sight of an intensely blue turquoise ring on Michael's finger. I had never seen it before, not because it was new, but because I had not yet been relaxed enough to look freely while in his office. I remember noticing how blue it was and asking about the ring, and seeing him smile before he told me about it, and feeling the warmth of our exchange. It was a small, and forgettable, moment, but one that I remember for its intimacy. I could never have orchestrated that interaction beforehand, as I often tried to do before going into his office, and that was the source of its power. I created the exchange out of what was available in that moment, and it was good. Therapy was like an infusion of that possibility into my life.

In the Buddha's psychological teachings the major obstacle

to this kind of spontaneous relating is called delusion. Delusion is the mind's tendency to seek premature closure about something. It is the quality of mind that imposes a definition on things and then mistakes the definition for the actual experience. Delusion would have me believe that I *was* my anxiety and that I was forever isolated as a result. Motivated by fear and insecurity, delusion creates limitation by imposing boundaries. In an attempt to find safety, a mind of delusion succeeds only in walling itself off.

In the world of psychotherapy this deluded quality of mind has not gone unnoticed, although it has been given different names. The French psychoanalyst Jacques Lacan pointed to it in his discussion of how the young child first catches sight of herself in the mirror and is enthralled by her image. The reflection becomes the ideal, thought Lacan. The British analyst D. W. Winnicott said much the same thing when he spoke of how the imposed coherence of the child's reactive mind obscures the capacity for spontaneity. What is lost in such a scenario, said Winnicott, is the capacity to be.

From D. W. Winnicott's perspective, "psychotherapy takes place in the overlap of two areas of playing, that of the patient and that of the therapist. . . . The corollary of this is that where playing is not possible then the work done by the therapist is directed towards bringing the patient from a state of not being able to play into a state of being able to play."[1] Another way of saying this is that therapy is a means of bringing someone from a state of not being able to relate into a state of relating. When I caught sight of Michael's ring and made mention of it, I was finally relating. It was a breakthrough for me, a recovery of a natural ability that had become dormant.

The relief that I felt at being able to engage in this way was nearly identical to the relief that I have at other times felt in meditation when making contact with my "big sky" mind. The two experiences have more than a superficial similarity. Both therapy and meditation, as disciplines, require the gentle coaxing and cajoling of the mind from a contracted state to a momentarily open and playful one.

When, in my first session, Michael made me aware of how little I was using my chair for support, he was trying to bring me into the state of being able to play. He had noticed one of the primary ways that I was restraining myself, one of the means by which I was keeping myself at bay. By sitting forward in my chair and giving myself no support, I was not in touch with my body. I was making a boundary between my mind and body that was limiting my experience. In the world of psychotherapy this is called a defense. I was trying to protect myself from anxiety by distancing myself from it.

stopping the wind

As we work to bring the lessons of meditation and psychotherapy to life, we see that this second, more active, aspect of surrender is as crucial as its receptive counterpart. Without the ability to meditate in action, it is all too easy to use the mental training of Buddhism or the self-knowledge of therapy to reinforce defenses instead of cutting through them.

The psychoanalyst Michael Eigen, for example, described his work with a young man named Ken who managed to use meditation to control, rather than transform, his mind. Ken was a meditator, married with children, whose ability to bring about calming internal states served as a much-needed antidote to a chaotic upbringing and a correspondingly chaotic psyche. When meditating, Ken felt calm and clear, filled with "such a fresh, unbreakable, full emptiness" that he emerged from his sitting clean and refreshed. His family, however, was loud and messy and disrespectful of his calm center. Their tumultuousness was beyond Ken's understanding or control.

"Part of Ken's difficulty," wrote Eigen, "was his hidden wish to control his family (perhaps life itself) with one mood." He could not go back and forth between stillness and storminess, between his one-pointed meditation and family life. "An unconscious severity structured his tranquillity. Meditation centered him, yet masked a tyrannical demand that life not be life, his wife not be his wife, his child not be his child."[2] He used meditation to keep himself from being immersed in the flow—and sometimes chaos—of his family life. He was like Freud's friends in the countryside in his inability to open to the tumultuous flow surrounding him. Having discovered his own still silent center, he was attempting to hold his family prisoner within his own quiet mind.

There is a story of the Abenaki Indians that my children like to listen to that parallels Ken's attempts to take the chaos out of his family life. It is about a curious young warrior, an ancestor from mythical times and something of a mischievous trickster, who sets out one day to stop the wind. He had been trying to paddle his canoe across the river, but the wind kept blowing him back, making it impossible for him to get to the other side. He goes after the wind, determined to find its source, and heads into it, hiking over vast stretches of land. After a long search, he finds it high on a mountain in the Adirondacks, in the form of an old wind-eagle whom he calls Grandfather. He tricks Grandfather into falling into a crevice between two mountains and thereby takes all movement out of the world. The weather gets hot, the ponds dry up and fill with scum, the fish and animals die, and the people are miserable. Stopping the wind makes everyone very uncomfortable.

In Tibetan Buddhism, and especially in the Tibetan medical system, "wind" is used as a metaphor for mind because both are in constant motion. Anyone with what we would call an emotional illness is said to have a "wind" disorder. There is a prominent wind disorder that afflicts meditators like Ken who try too hard to calm the mind, to force it into submission. The mind squeezes and tightens and "rises up" in rebellion at the attempts to subdue it, and the meditator gets more and more anxious and frustrated.

For the Abenaki people, their story is about how impossible it is to eliminate any one aspect of the world, no matter how angry it is making us. Movement is a part of creation, the wise Grandmother tells the impatient young hero as she convinces him to restore the wind-eagle to its proper place atop the mountain. The story applies equally well in a Buddhist context, or in a contemporary relationship one. Just as wind is a part of creation, so are anger, thoughts, or family turmoil. Stillness does not mean the elimination of disturbances as much as a different way of viewing them. If we can let anger rise and fall naturally, it becomes, in the Buddhist view, self-liberating. We get into trouble with anger if we try to eliminate it too precipitously, through denial or avoidance, or if we turn it into hatred.

As these stories suggest, using meditation or therapy to try to shut down parts of our experience is ultimately counterproductive. We do not have to be afraid of entering unfamiliar territory once we have learned how to meet experience with the gentleness of our own minds. Learning to transform obstacles into objects of meditation provides a much-needed bridge between the stillness of the concentrated mind and the movement of real life. As the practitioners of many martial arts often put it, we must learn to respond rather than react.

This is always the deeper meditative teaching. Rather than making a division between sacred and profane or between the spiritual and the everyday, the lesson of meditation is to bring awareness to bear on the (so-called) disturbances of everyday life. In Ken's case, this meant learning to be with his family's noisy messiness the same way one learns to incorporate street noise into the quiet of a concentrated mind. Rather than getting all worked up about how "that noise is disturbing *my* meditation," as I have done on many an occasion, I have learned to simply listen to the sounds of the garbage truck rising and falling in the space of my mind. Meditation can be practiced anywhere.

Thoughts do not have to be terminated through meditation; they can be simply observed. Disturbing emotions do not have to be excluded; they can be doorways into an aliveness that is as vivid as a moment of spontaneous laughter, or irritation. By learning to be with these emotions in a new way, we can, in fact, energize our lives and enrich our personal relationships. They give us access to ourselves, precisely because they challenge our attempts to keep ourselves together.

A longtime patient of mine, a woman in her mid-thirties named Alix, illustrated for me how important this understanding can be. When she was a young girl, Alix remembered, she taught herself how to blot out the sound of her parents' incessant fighting. She deliberately concentrated her mind "away" from the sound of their voices in the rough equivalent of a trance state. Like the young boy in Günter Grass's *The Tin Drum*, she managed to harness the power of her mind to eradicate that which she could not tolerate. The consequence of this maneuver, however, was that Alix had to recurrently rise above whatever emotional experience was taking place in her body into an isolated and safe haven in her mind. Her body was never really her own, and she was slow to develop a comfortable sexuality.

Alix's work in therapy was a restoration of her capacity for emotional experience. She needed to get her body back, and that meant (among other things) accepting how violently she could be repulsed by some things. She was not the "nice" person she had made herself out to be. When she could admit to her own negative reactions and could more easily tolerate being in her body, she was free to have a new experience there. Permitting herself the worst she could imagine, Alix opened up the possibility of going beyond it.

For Alix, therapy hinged on her ability to *remember* blotting out her parents' fighting. She had to look to the past in order to find out how it was that she prevented herself from being present. In finding out how uncomfortable she was with her own feelings, Alix became much less insulated. She discovered how she was perpetuating a method of adaptation (zoning out) that had in itself become a prison. This happened not through any interpretation on my part but through *awareness* of what she was doing to herself. Therapy created an environment, and a state of mind, in which Alix could discover that awareness on her own.

insulation

A friend of mine, the writer Stephen Batchelor, whose books on Buddhism, inspired by his years as a Tibetan and Zen monk, have done much to bring Buddhist thought to the West, described something similar to me about his own insulation. During his years as a Buddhist monk in Switzerland, he explained, he also entered into a form of Jungian therapy, called "Sandplay," with a noted Swiss analyst named Dora Kalff. He was drawn into therapy, he remembered, because he was still searching, even while being a monk, for a sense of personal authenticity that included creative self-expression. Within the monastic environment, Stephen found, this quality was rarely if ever encouraged.

Stephen came to therapy with "absolutely no idea what it was all about." Using a tableau of figurines, he constructed imaginative scenes in which he could act out all kinds of inter-personal and intrapsychic narratives. He was moved, he re-membered, by the "combination of freedom and safety" that his therapist was able to provide.

Although Stephen could appreciate that this combination of freedom and safety was linked to the state of mind cultivated in meditation, he found its expression in the psychotherapy office to be uncontaminated by the hierarchical dynamics that prevailed in the monasteries he had known. Batchelor found that in its emphasis on freeing his mind from the constraints of his day-to-day thought, psychotherapy's function, like that of meditation, was, for him, the *activation* of his imagination.[3] Psychotherapy helped him break through a layer of defensiveness that his monastic training had not touched. With his imagination so liberated, he found an aliveness that had otherwise escaped him.

The here and now of the psychotherapy ritual enabled Stephen to recover his mind's imaginative capacity. He had found himself to be unduly affected by the hierarchical restrictions prevailing in the monasteries that perhaps mimicked some early restrictive elements in his own childhood. All of us suffer from some kind of parallel limitations on our abilities to relate openly. As we discover these elements and learn to wend our way around them, we have the opportunity of touching the boundless expanse of our own minds and hearts.

There is a famous Tibetan story about a woman named Manibhadra[4] who attained enlightenment while carrying water from the village well back to her home. Dropping her pitcher one day and seeing the water gush out of the broken gourd, her consciousness was suddenly liberated. It flowed out of her and encompassed all of reality, revealing to Manibhadra how inseparable she was from her universe. This jarring loose, or breaking free, is what we are all seeking.

Buddhism teaches us that we are not so much isolated individuals as we are overlapping environments, and that we have the capacity to know ourselves in this way. In making a path through our own wilderness, we can discover what the Buddha called the "sure heart's release." No longer fearing isolation, we can surrender our need to be insulated. Like Manibhadra, we can discover how inexhaustible our hearts are when we let our unneeded defenses go to pieces.

p a r t   f o u r

ORGASM

bringing it all back home

X wants me to be there, beside him, while leaving him free *a little:* flexible, going away occasionally, but *not far:* on the one hand, I must be present as a prohibition (without which there would not be the right desire), but also I must go away the moment when, this desire having formed, I might be in its way: I must be the Mother who loves enough (protective and generous), around whom the child plays, while she peacefully knits or sews. This would be the structure of the "successful" couple: a little prohibition, a good deal of play; to designate desire and then to leave it alone, like those obliging natives who show you the path but don't insist on accompanying you on your way.

ROLAND BARTHES[1]

A LOVER'S DISCOURSE

7

passion

There is a saying in Buddhism that before we start practice, "mountains are mountains and rivers are rivers." Once we start to meditate, mountains are no longer mountains and rivers no longer rivers. Mountains seem like rivers, and rivers look like mountains. We lose our reference point and become less sure about who and what we are. With enough understanding, things click back into place: Mountains are once more mountains and rivers are once more rivers. This progression, simple though it is, conveys something of the remarkable trajectory that meditation launches.

When we begin practice, it is with a sense of the separateness of all things. I am me and you are you. The mountain is up here and the rivers are down below. We have to close ourselves off from the world in order to meditate. Thoughts and feelings seem to be distractions that must be eliminated.

Once we start to have some meditation experiences, the boundaries begin to break down. The ego starts to reveal its innate permeability. I am no longer so sure where I start and where you leave off. Mountains overlap with, and dissolve into, rivers. I discover that I cannot isolate myself from my world.

With enough practice, we can let things return to their preexisting states, but with the knowledge that everything is connected. The mountains exist in relationship to the rivers, and they make each other possible. I am still me and you are still you, but I know what kind of intimacy we are capable of. There is an inclusiveness in the new way of seeing that was not there originally. I no longer need to make thoughts or emotions the enemy but can make use of all aspects of my self to build my sacred space. I no longer have to push away disappointment; I can use it to develop my own tolerance. The separateness that I perceive does not have to obscure knowledge of my underlying connections. Daily life can be recast in the form of a mandala, the circular Buddhist image of sacred space.

This progression from mountains and rivers to mountains and rivers is a good metaphor for understanding how we can bring what we learn from meditation back to our lives. At first it seems as if we must, like the Buddha, renounce everything in order to find ourselves. And this willingness to renounce the seeking after pleasure is indeed a fundamental aspect of Buddhism. But once we start to appreciate how it is the holding on to pleasure and the pushing away of pain that is the problem (not pleasure and pain themselves), we start to see how it is possible to practice in the midst of our daily lives. Renunciation is not so compelling once we appreciate how truly impossible it is to renounce any aspect of an interdependent world.

Once we have this understanding it becomes possible to expand the field of meditation from our own inward journey to the rest of our lives. The very passions that once seemed so threatening to meditative stability can become special opportunities for self-discovery. Bringing the lessons of meditation back to daily life is one of the most important achievements we can hope for. It lies at the heart of the most beautiful and enduring visual symbol of Buddhism—the mandala.

mandala

A mandala is a sacred circle, a model or representation of an enlightened being or an undistracted mind. At the center sits a single Buddha figure, or sometimes a couple in a passionate embrace. It is one of the most ubiquitous symbols in the Buddhist world and is often used as an object of meditation or as an encapsulation of teachings on a certain subject. Its essential meaning, as the Buddhist scholar Robert A. F. Thurman has written, is as a depiction of liberation and bliss "by an individual fully integrated with his or her environment and field of associates."[2] The mandala is a description of how it is possible to remake our environments, seeing the everyday world through the joy of realization. It is a tangible demonstration of the fact that this very world of mountains and rivers is filled with the plenitude we seek. Each of us is already the mandala of our own liberation.

One of the most interesting aspects of the mandala is just how often the central image is of an entwined couple. Naturally, there are several meanings for this. On one level the copulating couple stands for the union of form and emptiness that underlies all of reality. On another level they represent the fusion of compassion and wisdom in the awakened mind. And on yet another level they refer back to the ordinary bliss of orgasm, which in Tibetan Buddhism is extolled as a window into the underlying and fundamental mind of pure being. If there is one moment when we drop our baggage and move away from the dominance of conceptual thought, teach the Tibetans, it is in orgasm. There are advanced meditation practices in Tibetan Buddhism, for instance, that actually use this sexual bliss as a vehicle for opening the mind.

As the imagery of the mandala suggests, there are important parallels between meditation and relationships. Just as I learned on retreat that my progress in meditation depended on my ability to bear disappointment, so too we discover that happiness in a relationship depends on the same capacity. Our lovers disappoint us just as our parents once did, but the mind, as Winnicott pointed out, is capable of tolerance.

In meditation, as in relationships, we can have experiences of profound harmony or union. The impulse in beginning meditation is to try to stop all thoughts and disturbing emotions, just as the impulse when falling in love is to try to preserve the harmony of the new couple. But stopping thoughts is about as effective as trying to have a relationship without fighting. The frustration that we feel with our lovers is mirrored by the frustration that many meditators feel with their own minds. In both cases, the most difficult thoughts and feelings are those involving the mix of desire and aggression.

While the mandala is supposed to be a sacred space that is undisturbed by distracting emotions, the critical question is about how to make such a space possible. While beginning meditation practices usually teach the value of subduing disturbances and quieting the mind, entering the mandala means finding another way. With enough practice in meditation we learn how to let disturbances come and go, turning them from obstacles into more grist for the mill. This is the key to the mandala. When we learn to let emotions like anger rise and fall on their own, instead of struggling to get rid of them, we can deepen our practice and enhance our capacities for relationship and passionate engagement.

If we are unwilling to make room for our most unruly

feelings, we must shut ourselves down instead. The ability to not be unnerved by such powerful emotions seems to be related to the capacity to be alone. One of the things I have learned from my patients is that those people who are least secure in their aloneness have the most trouble with the pressures of intimacy. They seem to view the elimination of separateness as the desirable goal of a relationship, just as many people engaged in meditation see the elimination of disturbing emotions as the pinnacle of spiritual understanding. Yet this is a recipe for disaster.

sexual yoga

The mandala implies that all of our experience can be enlightening. In its liberal use of the imagery of desire and aggression, it suggests that there is another way of working with the passions than trying to eliminate them, or than simply being controlled by them. To understand what the mandala promises, we need to know a bit more about the central couple, about how sexual relations are understood from the perspective of Tibetan Buddhism.

In the sexual yoga of Buddhism the passion of amorous relations is harnessed as a means of converting the more familiar energy of doing into the more subtle, but ultimately more powerful and enlightening, energy of being. Sexual relations serve both as a vivid model for the spiritual journey and as a reminder of how much is lost when the spiritual dimension of sexuality is neglected.

In its recognition of how spiritual the process of lovemaking can be, the Tibetan practices remind us of something that our culture, with all of its sexual freedom and supposed uninhibition, is in danger of losing. Just as someone who is sexually abused or degraded in her early sexual encounters has trouble opening up to the potentially transcendent nature of sexual intimacy, so too our culture, with its aggressive promulgation of sexuality, has difficulty cultivating the more subtle but powerful energy of passionate intimacy. While even Freud recognized that falling in love was one of those mystical times of ego dissolution, we have had trouble realizing how exalted a state this really is.

The practice of sexual tantra is built upon the truth that clinging is as much of a problem in lovemaking as in the rest of life. In order for sexual relations to be deeply satisfying, there must be a yielding of this clinging in a manner that actually affirms the unknowability and separateness of the loved partner. It is the peculiar convergence of awe and appreciation with pleasure and release that characterizes the best sexual experiences. Separate and together cease to be mutually exclusive and instead become, in psychoanalyst Christopher Bollas's phrase, "reciprocally enhancing and mutually informative."[3] There is wisdom in this state, not just raw instinct.

In the Tibetan traditions of sexual tantra, it is understood that our usual ways of approaching sexual relations are not the most direct route to this wisdom. While these practices are cloaked in secrecy, their outlines have become much more available in recent years.[4] They suggest that, while most of us will never become full-fledged practitioners of sexual yoga, that there are certain guidelines that we can all benefit from. In many ways, these guidelines speak to just the issues that many of us face in our relationships.

In sexual tantra, it is understood that most of our standard sexual conventions must stand on their heads. The male partner is encouraged to admit his dependence upon his lover, to continually subordinate his need to dominate or control, and to develop a reverent attitude toward the woman's unfathomable arousal. "Her lap is the sacrificial altar," reads one secret text, "her hair, the sacrificial grass."[5] Meanwhile, lovers are taught to breathe their genital feelings upward, dispersing them throughout body and mind instead of localizing them in the genitals. The intertwined couple are taught to spin a mandala palace of great bliss between them, like spiders spinning a web.

In the culmination of practice, the man is urged to absorb the female sexual secretion in orgasm. Completely reversing the usual state of affairs in which the man ejaculates into the woman, the lovers are taught to do something different, to rest instead in the female response. No longer responsible for "giving" his partner an orgasm, the man simply becomes part of it. While turning his own organs and fluids into offerings, the man is encouraged to receive the mysterious female essence as the culmination of the sexual act. Drinking this nectar of pure being, couples are able to realize the union of bliss and emptiness. "This is the best diet," reads the Candamaharosana Tantra, "eaten by all Buddhas."[6]

In their own way, the sexual tantras affirm the more traditional view of meditation, painting it with a different brush. Our habitual ways of thinking and doing obscure the underlying reality, they suggest. Just as most couples engage in sexual activity without realizing how much more subtle and all-pervasive their pleasure could be, so do we go through our lives without experiencing much of the joy that is available through the simple nonactivity of being. Just as the sexual yogi has to learn to stop doing and make himself into an offering so that he can appreciate the profundity of his partner's arousal, so too do we have to learn how to stop proving ourselves and surrender to the more magnificent world of which we are a part.

The liberal use of sexual imagery in the center of the mandala drives home the message about reinvigorating daily life with the wisdom of meditation. All of the passions can be transformed, the mandalas teach. We can take what we learn from spiritual practice and make use of it in our relationships. We do not have to separate our intimate emotional lives from our spiritual ones. In my work as a therapist with people who come to me with difficulties in relationships, I am often struck by how useful the mandala imagery can be in finding a way of working through these difficulties. Just as in the mandala, the key is always in finding another way of dealing with the most disturbing difficulties.

the goddess at the doorway

Richard Kohn, a Buddhist scholar and art historian, made a discovery while doing research in Nepal on Tibetan Buddhist art and ritual that has helped me immeasurably in working with my patients on relationship issues.[7] He found that certain mandalas and Buddhist temples shared a surprising feature. Standing at the doorways of the temple at the periphery of the circle, representing the transition point between an unenlightened and an enlightened state of mind, Kohn discovered a curious set of figures: animal-headed goddesses striking sexually provocative poses, guarding the entrances to the sacred space. Kohn became intrigued with these figures. What were they doing there? What could they represent? What were the Buddhists of one thousand years ago saying about what it took to awaken the mind?

As he examined the temple goddesses more closely, he began to decode them. With voluptuous female bodies and heads of birds or beasts of prey, they represented transitional figures, neither human nor animal, sacred nor profane. Standing in a sexually aggressive posture, each figure held a set of implements that symbolized the meditator being seduced and overcome. The four instruments—a hook that draws in, a lasso that ties up, a chain that binds, and a maddening bell—together represent the ritual acts of summoning, tying, binding, and intoxicating.

There appeared to be a double meaning to this visual language. The successful meditator must tame passion and be tamed by it, he must invoke the deity that he wishes to merge with at the center of the mandala and also be overcome by it. In psychological terms, he must "pass through" the kinds of difficult emotions that such an animal-headed goddess could provoke, just as in physical terms he would have to pass through these figures in order to gain access to the sanctity of the temple complex.

I thought of these goddess figures when working with a patient of mine, a thirty-eight-year-old artist named Joe, who despaired of ever being able to marry his current girlfriend. An appealing and accomplished man with a long history of emotionally engaged relationships that had yielded both much exaltation and much sorrow, Joe had come to a point where he knew too much about himself to enter into a new relationship without already seeing the seeds of his own discontent.

A passionate lover and devotee of female beauty and charm, Joe was never happier than when he was caught up in the excitement of a new relationship. But when that relationship stopped being perfect, when his partner lost her temper once too often, became emotionally unavailable, showed selfishness or immaturity, or became less than totally admiring, Joe would become so frustrated and angry that he would turn from a sensitive lover into a teasing older brother and gradually undermine the trust of the relationship. Enraged and resentful at his lover's withholding, Joe found it impossible to maintain his passion for her. His aggression led him to become sexually frustrated and demanding instead of energized and appreciative. His relationships collapsed under the weight of his own outrage, and he remained frustratingly disoriented within the labyrinth of his own passions. His current relationship seemed to be following just such a scenario.

Joe, I decided, was having trouble getting in the door of his own mandala. He was being obstructed by his anger. He had not yet found a way of using his passion to tame his anger, nor was he able to subvert his resentment into the cause of desire. The animal-headed goddesses were emblematic of a transformation that Joe had not figured out. As transition figures from outside the mandala to the inside, they symbolized the possibility of using anger to find bliss. But for Joe, they were still blocking his access to the central couple.

One of the principles of the mandala is that all of the outer phenomena actually unfold from the center, as petals do from the interior of a flower. While the center represents the purest and most concentrated version of the mandala's energy, the peripheral manifestations nonetheless carry the seed of that purity. Thus, the temple goddesses embody both the seductive and the aggressive energy necessary for the passion of the central couple. To reach the center, one had to first become the periphery. Joe was having trouble tapping this energy, however. He could not locate the goddess, nor could he become her. He was locked into his anger and resentment and could not admit that behind that anger lay desire for the very women whom he felt betrayed by.

recruiting aggression

In his book on sexual intimacy, *Love Relations*, the psychoanalyst Otto Kernberg observed that the most important missing ingredient in an otherwise satisfactory but sexually uninvigorating relationship is what he called "polymorphous perverse infantile sexuality."[8] While this is an old concept in psychoanalysis, it is usually used to describe the early sexualized behavior of young children. Kernberg was talking specifically about adults, about the aggressive components of sexual excitement that can permit a couple to "recruit aggression in the service of love."[9] This is what Joe needed help in permitting. By becoming locked into his anger, Joe became stuck in it. He could not stay fluid enough in his responses to blend his anger into his desire. He kept the two emotions separate, and he isolated himself as a result.

The sexual arena is one in which the frustrations of separateness can be calmed and the resentments of disappointment drowned. It is an environment in which the most primitive, and taboo, impulses—of sucking, biting, teasing, prohibition, and surrender—can be acted out in the pursuit of union. Just as a child needs her fears held and calmed in her mother's understanding, so too a lover needs her clamor for reunion contained by a passionate response. Passion is a vehicle for containing the incendiary mix of anger and desire. Anger loses its aversive quality and becomes raw excitement. As lovers attack each other's boundaries and gradually yield to each other's desire, they enter a territory in which the emotions of separateness pulse as one.

In my role as therapist, I saw the lovers at the heart of the mandala as the embodiment of mature sexual love that was able to fuse tenderness, passion, love, and erotic desire. From a Buddhist perspective, I knew that they symbolized a more generalized version of this capacity, the ability to bring the bliss of orgasm to bear on the everyday world. For Joe, neither of these lofty goals were achievable because of his inability to get through the outer doorway. He could not approach the copulating figures at the center without getting derailed by his own resentment. The metaphoric goddesses were not letting him pass.

While I never used the mandala imagery directly with Joe, I did focus attention on his anger and resentment. Joe was letting his anger get in the way of his ultimate satisfaction: He was using it as a reason to avoid marriage. The mandala principle suggested that this was unnecessary, as did the experts on mature sexual love like Dr. Kernberg. Joe needed to learn a different way of relating to his angry responses. As we talked about this, Joe discovered why these particular emotions were so difficult. His earliest memories were of being told what he was feeling by his intrusive mother, whose controlling ways permeated his family's dynamics. She would feed him dinner but unilaterally override his protestations of being full and force him to eat until he felt sick. "I'm full, I'm full!" he would scream, but she would yell back, "No, you're not! You'll be hungry again in an hour."

Joe's older sisters took up their mother's mantle and perpetuated his distrust of controlling women. Joe's father never really distinguished himself in his work, surrendering to a dependent reliance on his wife's business acumen. Joe grew up secretly vowing never to succumb to a woman's power as he had seen his father do. He wanted at all costs, he would say, to avoid appearing weak or dependent.

There is no way to experience desire, however, without yielding some amount of control. By its very nature, desire affirms that the loved person is just slightly out of reach and that we *need* them. Most of us have had the experience of too much availability diminishing desire. For Joe, this was a big problem. He found that he unconsciously resented whomever he was most attracted to because of the power that his desire conferred on them. He envied their ability to tempt him.

When they disappointed him, which was virtually inevitable, his resentment would flower into rage and he would become self-righteous or spiteful. He was so vigilant in avoiding dependency that he never learned how to work with these emotions.

Complicating this picture, Joe started to see, was the fact that he did his best to choose girlfriends who were nothing like his mother or sisters. When confronted by his rage, these women, who had, as a rule, grown up in repressed households with very little display of aggression, became frightened and withdrawn. They were not able to help Joe with his anger because they were so intimidated by it. They could not be his goddess at the doorway, summoning, tying, binding, and intoxicating Joe's aggression. Joe's compromise was to favor relationships that hinged on his being admired, but that did not involve much in the way of reciprocity. Joe could be at the center of the mandala by himself but not in the company of another.

One of the consequences of this situation was that Joe was unable to make use of the anger and resentment that inevitably shadowed his desire. As we talked about this, I began to see that Joe feared that his anger would destroy his girlfriend. He was withdrawing, not just out of frustration, but out of fear that she could not tolerate how bad he was. This led him to withhold his aggression in the sexual arena as well, so that, as a couple, they were never given a chance to transmute anger through passion. Joe did not have faith in his girlfriend's love for him. He did not believe that her love could survive his aggression. But he was not giving her a chance. In his desire to avoid such a confrontation, Joe attempted to control his lover just as he imagined his mother had once controlled him. He wanted everything to be perfect in his relationship, but when it could not be, he withdrew. In order for Joe to actually enter into the mandala he had to first learn how to work with the disturbing feelings that were aroused by his lover's autonomy.

In Otto Kernberg's pioneering work on mature sexual love, he made much of this capacity to tolerate one's lover's separateness. "The beloved," he made clear, "presents himself or herself simultaneously as a body which can be penetrated and a consciousness which is impenetrable." There is always an element of separation in even the most profound union. "Love is the revelation of the other person's freedom,"[10] he concluded. This revelation is almost always painful because it confronts our most possessive desires.

beyond attunement

Just as a mind rises up and rebels at an unskillful attempt to subdue it in meditation, a relationship will fall apart if the partners are not respectful of each other's differences. No matter how much we yearn for complete attunement, this is not what we need. Just as a young child needs to be left on her own in the presence of her mother so that she can discover her own vast unknowability, so too we continue to need that freedom to be alone in the midst of our intimacy. It is that continuing unknowability that fuels a relationship. While there can be intense pressure in a couple to override differences and to eliminate separateness, the insistence on complete attunement has a suffocating effect. Attraction is based in otherness and difference as much as it depends on recurrent harmony or satisfaction. Separateness and connection make each other possible; they are not mutually exclusive.

Like Freud's friends, who shrunk back from the terrifying transitoriness of the flower's bloom, and like Joe, we recoil from the revelation of our lover's freedom. We insist on holding on, or we withdraw prematurely, rather than trusting in love's ability to constantly reassert itself. Yet this is precisely what makes a relationship as much of a spiritual teaching as a classical meditation. Both confront us with our refusal to let go, with our expectations for how things are supposed to be. Both demand faith that we will survive our own worst impulses. Both reveal the essential unknowability of self and other while at the same time providing a means of revelling in it.

The temple goddesses at the doorway of the mandala have a lot to teach us about the harnessing of primitive aggression and frustration in the service of passion and appreciation. "It is not such a long stretch from disappointment to empathy,"[11] wrote my therapist Michael Vincent Miller in his book *Intimate Ter-*

rorism, some years after I had completed my work with him. We must find a way of bringing those very feelings of outrage and envy that are the inevitable consequence of our lover's freedom into the service of our relationships. Tantric Buddhism makes such liberal use of the sexual metaphor because the methods employed in passion and in meditation to convert disappointment into empathy are so similar. Rather than treating such feelings as enemies to be defeated, both require learning how to summon, tie, bind, and intoxicate like the goddesses at the temple doors.

While I was working with Joe on passing through the doorways of the temple goddesses, my son had a dream of being mauled by a huge tiger. He woke up his sister and she comforted him, and he told me about it the next morning as I was getting myself ready for an appointment with Joe.

"Try making friends with that tiger," I suggested offhandedly to my son. "He might have a present for you or something."

"I heard a voice in the dream, Daddy," my son then told me. "From someone who wasn't there. It said, 'Look into its eyes.'"

My son's dream message was the key to Joe's predicament. Rather than avoiding the disturbing mix of desire and aggression that the goddesses represented, Joe had to look into their eyes. With their voluptuous bodies, their provocative stance, and their bird-of-prey features, they perfectly embodied the mix of feelings that Joe's girlfriend had engendered in him. Intolerant of how frustrated her otherness was making him, Joe had shut down his love and inhibited his desire. He had stopped idealizing her the way he once had because it made him too insecure to adore someone who could be so disappointing.[12]

Joe was reluctant to admit that this was how it had to be. His love for his girlfriend meant that he could not be in complete control. Given this predicament, there was no way to avoid feeling vulnerable, and no way to avoid feeling angry or hurt. Worse yet, there was no way to be absolutely sure that she could tolerate him. But Joe's aggression did not have to be such a threat. If he could let his anger rise and fall without shutting down, if he could submerge his outrage in the passion of his sexual relations, if he could admit to envying the very person whom he so needed, then his relationship could survive. By looking into his goddess's eyes, Joe could experience his love in all of its terrifying splendor. It was not what he thought it should be, but it was real.

8
relief

There is a story from the Buddha's time about a house-holder named Nakulapita who went to the Buddha for advice on peace of mind. "I am old and decrepit," he told the Bud-dha. "I am sick and constantly ailing. My body hurts all the time. What can I do to find happiness?"

The Buddha took Nakulapita's complaints seriously. "Even so," he said to him right away. (The Buddha often said, "Even so." Like a good psychotherapist, he tended to agree with his patients' self-assessments, even when they might wish them to be challenged.) "It is true, Nakulapita. Your body is old and sick. With a body like yours, even a moment of good health would be a miracle. Therefore, you should train yourself like this: 'Though I am ill in body, my mind shall not be ill.'"

Nakulapita felt refreshed by this possibility. His body was going to pieces but he did not have to fall apart. He went to one of the Buddha's chief disciples, Sariputta, for further instruction.

Sariputta built upon the Buddha's lesson in his subsequent teachings. "Do not look upon your body as your self," he told Nakulapita. "Do not think that the body is the self or that the self is the body, or that the self is in the body or that the body is in the self. Do not look upon your feelings as your self, your thoughts as your self, even your consciousness as your self. Your body can change and become otherwise," he told him, "but grief, lamentation, pain, dejection, and despair do not have to arise."[1]

Sariputta was teaching something very radical, that it was possible to let the mind float free of identifications with any aspect of the mind-body process. This is a point that the Tibetan Buddhists of many centuries later have also made in their secret teachings about orgasm and death. In both processes, the Tibetans teach, the self is swallowed up in the intensity of the experience. If we do not resist, we have the opportunity to glimpse this freely floating mind.

But the Tibetans believe that we are all afraid of this loss of self and that we unconsciously pull back from a complete immersion in the mind that peeks through in such situations. Even in sex, they say, we resist completely losing ourselves, while in death we are notoriously fearful. But they also believe, as the Buddha and Sariputta did, that it is possible to train the mind to sustain its awareness so that the bliss that naturally dawns in orgasm and in death can shine through and permeate our regular lives. Thus, while teaching the emptiness of all things (no self in the body, no self in feelings or thoughts, no self in consciousness), Buddhists also teach a positive emptiness, a luminous knowing that is sometimes called the clear light nature of mind. This is the mind that the Buddha was pointing out to Nakulapita, the mind that holds the key to relief.

the three messengers

In approaching old age, illness, and death we are all faced with the need for a mind that can withstand disintegration. Our usual strategies of managing threats to our self-sufficiency do not work very well in these situations. We are trained to keep ourselves together, but we do not get much teaching in falling apart. My own grandfather, whom I never knew, handed down to me a good lesson about this.

An intensely competent high school principal in Brooklyn, my grandfather Max was raised in South Carolina by parents who embraced a highly principled philosophy that seemed to have Victorian roots. Every morning he would study a kind of moral catechism that stressed the writings and sayings of great men, and he lived by these ethics as well as anyone might. He proudly taught my father, whom he had named after Benjamin Franklin, to read at the age of two, stringing flash cards down the staircase so that my father could sit at the bottom of the stairs and watch the letters of the alphabet come fluttering down to him. He had a huge workbench full of tools in his basement and fingers that were crooked from years of playing catcher in semiprofessional baseball leagues.

Several years after insulating the attic of his home, he developed a malignant tumor of the lungs that was caused by inhaling fragments of the newly marketed asbestos fibers that he was using. Treated at home for as long as possible, he received regular injections of morphine for his pain that my father, at the age of sixteen, learned how to administer. Yet through all of this he never told his wife what he himself knew: that he was dying. Protecting my grandmother from the pain of his own death, he never permitted her to hug him good-bye.

Despite my grandfather's moral backbone and intellectual accomplishments, he was unable or unwilling to face the reality of his impending death with my grandmother. Perhaps he was attempting to protect her, the way one wishes one could do for a child. My grandmother never really knew. She was left to struggle with feeling betrayed by the person whom she had loved most in the world. And her pain, judging from the tears shed fifty years later as she told me her story, had not abated in the interim.

In the story of the Buddha's life there was a similar situation. After his mother's death in childbirth, the Buddha-to-be
grew up in a royal household in which any hints of old age,
illness, or death were prohibited by his father's decree. Suckled
by wet nurses and raised in the most privileged surroundings of
his day, young Gautama was kept isolated from any whisper of
death. Out riding in the countryside one day, he chanced
upon an old person, a sick person, and a corpse—sights he had
never before seen. The feelings aroused in him by these sights
were so disturbing that they prompted him to forsake all that
his father had created for him. He left his palace and his family
and began a search for peace of mind. He later called those
images of old age, illness, and death the "three messengers"
that awaken people to the spiritual life.

"Did you ever see in the world a man, or a woman, eighty,
ninety, or a hundred years old," asked the Buddha in a famous
talk many years later, "frail, crooked as a gable-roof, bent
down, resting on crutches, with tottering steps, infirm, youth
long since fled, with broken teeth, gray and scanty hair or
none, wrinkled, with blotched limbs? And did the thought
never come to you that you also are subject to decay, that you
also cannot escape it?"[2]

The Buddha's father did everything for him except provide
him with a forum to explore death. Like my grandfather, he
hoped to spare his loved ones the pain of this reality, but as the
Buddha discovered, this is not a viable approach. It is much

better to confront the truth head on. Indeed, in the Buddhist meditative tradition it was not unusual for beginning meditators to spend extended periods meditating on the bodies of corpses in cremation grounds, sitting with the emotions that arise when confronted with such stark reality.

the clear light nature of mind

In Buddhism, it is understood that meditation is practice for death. The ability to open one's mind to the unstructured reality that is beyond identification with mind and body is seen as the crucial link between dying and practice. In the secret Tibetan traditions, advanced meditation practices actually involve simulating the dissolution of consciousness that takes place at death so that the yogi can gain experience with the mind of clear light. These are very complicated practices that are engaged in only after years of preparatory study and meditation.

For many years, I was unsure if these practices were still alive or if they existed only in the esoteric books I was fond of reading. But by the time I was done with medical school, through a curious set of circumstances, I had come face to face with Tibetan monks in India who were the masters of these techniques.

During my time in college and medical school I would occasionally drop by the office of Herbert Benson, a cardiologist at the Harvard Medical School for whom I had worked one summer after my sophomore year in college. Dr. Benson was responsible for some of the earliest and best physiological documentation of the benefits of meditation. His book, *The Relaxation Response*, published in 1975, described this research and introduced the notion of meditation as effective for relieving stress. Dr. Benson and I traded ideas about medicine, meditation, and life in general.

During one of these meetings, Dr. Benson asked me if I had ever read the reports of the French explorer Alexandra David-Neel from the beginning of the century about her experiences in Tibet. *Magic and Mystery in Tibet* was the most well known of her texts. I was familiar with the books but had not read them. Dr. Benson wanted to know if I had ever heard of any of the "miracles" that she reported encountering: monks who could fly or who could raise their body temperatures to the point where they could sit outside in freezing temperatures and dry wet sheets with the heat of their naked bodies. I confessed that I had not but told him that I had heard that the Dalai Lama was planning a trip to the East Coast shortly, and I thought that if we went through the appropriate channels, we could ask him ourselves.

We went through those channels and several months later, in the fall of 1979, found ourselves face-to-face with the Dalai Lama. Dr. Benson spoke of his curiosity and of the potential benefits of documenting such prodigious accomplishments if indeed they existed. The Dalai Lama acknowledged the existence of the "heat yoga" practices, stressed their secrecy and the potential for misunderstanding what they were all about, but seemed interested in the possibility of allowing Western science to document the "inner science" of his religion and culture.

It was not too long before I found myself part of a research team in Dharamsala, India, inserting rectal probes into the bodies of slightly bemused but cooperative monks who were interrupting their years of solitary retreat in cabins in the Himalayan foothills to participate in our project. Under the auspices of the Dalai Lama, our research team hiked to the remote cabins of three yogis and subjected them to a battery of tests as they meditated. The monks, whose good humor and serenity were palpable even as we made our measurements, were indeed doing something extraordinary. They were able to reach inside their involuntary nervous systems and gain control of the mechanisms that regulated their peripheral body temperatures. They could sit in their unheated cabins dressed only in the thinnest of cotton robes and keep themselves warm no matter how cold it was outside.

We wrote up our findings in a scholarly journal[3] and proudly discussed them for the national news media upon our return, but we were really seeing only a fraction of what these monks were accomplishing. Our approach was rather like investigating the existence of an automobile by measuring its exhaust or that of a dog by studying the wagging of its tail. Indeed, these monks were engaged in practices designed to open their minds to a luminosity that our scientific instruments have not yet found a way to measure. Their ability to affect their involuntary nervous systems was an outward sign of a more profound inner transformation. They were learning to simulate death and to saturate their minds with the bliss of an extended orgasm.[4] In so doing, as the Buddha suggested to Nakulapita, they were eradicating every last vestige of fear of old age, illness, and death. The relief that comes from this fearlessness was wonderful to see.

It was, of course, easier for us to talk about physiological changes than spiritual ones. It can be difficult for the uninitiated to get a clear sense of what the mind that dawns in death or in orgasm could possibly be like. One of the best descriptions that I have found comes from a dream reported by Heinz Pagels, a Rockefeller University quantum physicist and avid mountain climber who was killed in a mountaineering accident in 1988.

"I often dream about falling," wrote Pagels in his book *The Cosmic Code.* "Such dreams are commonplace to the ambitious or those who climb mountains. Lately I dreamed I was clutching at the face of a rock, but it would not hold. Gravel gave way. I grasped for a shrub, but it pulled loose, and in cold terror I fell into the abyss. Suddenly I realized that my fall was relative; there was no bottom and no end. A feeling of pleasure overcame me. I realized that what I embody, the principle of life, cannot be destroyed. It is written into the cosmic code, the order of the universe. As I continued to fall in the dark void, embraced by the vault of the heavens, I sang to the beauty of the stars and made my peace with the darkness."[5]

What Pagels described is a beautiful evocation of the kind of mind that arises naturally in meditation as the usual identifications with more superficial aspects of the self are stripped away. It is negative in the sense of there being nothing to hold on to, but positive in the sense of there being an underlying conscious life energy that is luminous and knowing. In Buddhist psychology, this underlying and more subtle consciousness is known to be more powerful than the grosser minds of thought and sensory consciousness that usually dominate our awareness. It is known to be more powerful not because it has been measured, but because it has been felt.

luminous knowing

It is the function of meditation to make this knowledge accessible and incontrovertible. The mind, taught the Buddha, is like a nugget of gold. Before it is worked on, it does not look like much, but if you know what to do with it, you can make it shine. The mind that realizes its own Buddha nature is said to be like clear space—it is empty and all-pervasive but also vividly aware.[6] These two qualities, of knowing and spaciousness, correspond to the positive and negative aspects of empti-ness. In the Buddhist teachings they are inextricably linked, united in the center of the mandala in an ecstatic embrace, creating the field in which the phenomenal world takes form.

This luminous nature of mind, while underlying our every-day experience the way the quantum universe underlies the material one, is useful to us only if it is acknowledged. Most of the time, because it challenges our conventional view of things and our need for security, we refuse to take note of this di-mension of reality. Only very occasionally, maintain the Ti-betan "inner scientists," during uncontrolled events like sneez-ing, fainting, going to sleep, ending a dream, having an orgasm, or dying, does this clear light nature of mind shine through our everyday consciousness.[7] Most of the time, our habits are such that we ignore these brief openings and climb back immediately into the daily world of our defenses. We do not take refuge in the relief that is available to us.

The Tibetan monks whom we studied were actually prac-ticing keeping their minds in these openings, using techniques of esoteric meditation to manifest and dwell within their minds of clear light. Their practices were related to the more well-known *Tibetan Book of the Dead*, in which the dying per-son is counselled not to identify with the various fears that arise in the process of dying but to yield to the mind that underlies conventional reality.

It was the cultivation of this mind of pure awareness that

distinguished the esoteric practices that the Dalai Lama permitted us to investigate in the Himalayas. But it was not necessary to travel all the way to India to discover the positive side of emptiness, nor did I need to engage in the most esoteric Buddhist practices to become convinced of its accessibility. Just as the Tibetans found that the clear light nature of mind shines through whenever we let go of identification with the mind's content, so have I found that this silent center of the human personality can manifest in the most mundane situations. Whether it is revealed in lovemaking, meditation, or psychotherapy, this unstructured and unintegrated state of mind is the foundation of all that is healing.

Like meditation, psychotherapy has the potential to reveal how much of our thinking is an artificial construction designed to help us cope with an unpredictable world. And like meditation, therapy can show us how much we identify with our thinking minds, the way Nakulapita identified with his deteriorating body. What therapy can also offer is a window into that liberating state of mind that comes from the absence of identification. This happens most often in those moments when we are least sure of just what therapy is supposed to be doing.

"Why keep coming to therapy if I have nothing to say?" we ask, with the same fears that the Tibetans notice in the face of death. We worry, thinking, "I don't know what to talk about," not realizing that such moments are the threshold of the relief we are seeking. The idea of surrendering to a fertile silence, like yielding to an unpredictable arousal, is threatening to a brittle self that is secretly protecting an untouched and long-forgotten soul. Only very occasionally can we float free in the abyss, as Dr. Pagels described.

There is an apocryphal tale of James Joyce asking Carl Jung what the difference was between his own mind and that of his schizophrenic daughter that illustrates this point.

"She falls," Jung is said to have replied. "You jump!"

I unexpectedly had a sense of this on another meditation retreat. I was in western Massachusetts during a very cold February, sitting silently over a ten-day period. Every day after lunch, instead of taking my customary nap, I decided to put on five layers of clothing and walk in the surrounding countryside for an hour. I tried to time my excursions to be back in time for the first afternoon meditation. The winter had been filled with snowstorms, and the rural forests and farmlands surrounding the meditation center had taken on the ghostly and sparkling look of Alaskan tundra.

Each day I would walk briskly and meditatively with my eyes down and my attention focused on my body's movements. There were empty roads and paths leading every which way so that after thirty minutes I would always be in a completely different place. At that point I would stop and look around with the full force of my concentrated awareness before turning and heading back.

The first day I found myself in the middle of a frozen lake with a windstorm swirling the snow in circles about me. The second day I was halfway up a hill looking up at the sky at the instant that the first flakes of a new snowfall came fluttering down in slow motion on to my upturned face. The next day I was standing silently in the middle of a completely still forest when, with a sudden whoosh, an owl swooped low over my head with one huge dark wing extended.

I began to think there was something awesome about my timing. How was it that, at the exact moment of my stopping, such incredible things were happening? It took me longer than I am prepared to admit to realize that such things were *always* happening. It was only that I was finally paying attention.

These walks taught me much about the function of meditation. My practice was like the methodical thirty-minute walk. It could take me somewhere, but I had to remember to look around once I got there. Those moments of silent awareness in the forest were precious because of how open and connected I felt. Rather than feeling one with the universe, I still felt my own presence, yet my experience of myself was altered. Like a child whose mind is free to roam because he is secure in his mother's presence, I completely let down my guard. I had the awareness of just how unimportant my efforts to understand myself were. Relaxing my mind into its own deeper nature, as I was doing spontaneously when I interrupted my walk, I could reach beyond my personality into something more open.

Like meditation, psychotherapy can be a vehicle for this kind of reappraisal. It, too, can seem like a long walk that suddenly opens up into an extraordinary vision of something that has always been available but has been unrecognized. A longtime patient of mine, with whom I worked for about ten years, elucidated for me how psychotherapy can function in this manner. Greta came to see me every week as she navigated work and family issues, successfully raising three children alone while working a full-time job. She wanted therapy because she felt lonely and because she was vaguely aware of how judgmental she was toward most people in her life. When disappointed or hurt by someone, Greta's tendency was to write them off forever. She could be quite unforgiving.

Over the years we developed a very strong connection which was probably responsible for Greta's staying with therapy for such a long time. In the midst of her highly pressured life she felt the sessions to be an oasis of mostly positive feeling, despite the occasional bothersome realization of my inaccessible private life. My impetus in our sessions was always to give Greta space, to open up the cracks between issues or between thoughts and to see what was there. I found a great deal of feeling, some of it loving and appreciative and some of it angry.

My work with Greta felt like untangling my daughter's knotted hair or like untying a fine gold chain. I would get one little strand free, open up a little space, and then start working on the next piece. As I proceeded in this manner, Greta became more and more able to freely express her resentful feelings toward me. One evening, after having been at my office that afternoon, she was struck by a huge wave of love for me that made her feel very peaceful. She was having extraordinarily positive feelings for me without wanting anything back. That evening she had two dreams.

In the first, Greta dreamed of herself with her father when she was three or four years old and felt with great conviction the unconflicted love she had for him at that time. Since Greta had only spoken of her father in the most unfavorable terms, finding him to be pompous, self-centered, and boorish, this was a major surprise to both of us. Coming out of the first dream, Greta had one question. Where had this love gone?

The second dream answered the question. Again Greta dreamed of her father, but this time she heard herself yelling at him.

"Can't you shut up?" she screamed in her dream. "You're talking at me all the time. I don't know my own thoughts. I don't even know who I am."

Greta remembered how relentlessly her father had pursued her as she grew up, how attached he was to her love, and how needy he was for reassurance.

"He wouldn't leave me alone," she told me regretfully.

Greta's father would become irate whenever she disappointed him, and she finally had to close herself off from him in order to find some peace. In the next session after her dreams, Greta confirmed something that is the key to both Buddhism and psychotherapy.

"The defense is what hurt," she told me.

In protecting herself from her father's intrusive neediness, Greta had erected an unforgiving veneer that had interfered with her ability to find fulfillment as an adult. This was the defense to which she referred. While Greta needed to close herself off to her love for her father in order to find herself, she also needed to recover her love in order to be whole. Without this recovery, Greta could know herself only as an angry woman. Our therapy relationship had untangled enough of that defense for Greta to open her heart to me and then to dream of the love that had been hiding. Made inaccessible by her father's overbearing intrusiveness, this love was the underlying reality from which she had been estranged. As she worked her way around the defense, getting to know it in her relationship with me, the love that it had obscured came flooding back.

Many weeks later Greta came to my office and pointed to

her head with a smile. "It's so quiet in here now," she sighed contentedly.

In her realization that the defense is what hurts, Greta was, in her own way, articulating the central concept of this book. In coping with the world, we come to identify only with our compensatory selves and our reactive minds. We build up our selves out of our defenses but then come to be imprisoned by them. This leaves us feeling dissatisfied, irritable, and cut off. In our misguided attempts to become more self-assured, we tend to build up our defenses even more, rather than disentangling ourselves from them. We use therapy to apportion blame rather than to learn tolerance. This gives us a bigger and better self but not a truer or happier one. It only exacerbates the problem.

Greta's breakthrough relates to an old Zen story that has done much to inform my own practice. An aged Chinese monk, after many years of practice without deep realization, went to his master and asked for permission to go off into the mountains to seek enlightenment in an isolated cave. His master, seeing the monk's sincerity, urged him on his way. Taking his robes, his begging bowl, and a few possessions, the monk headed out on foot through the neighboring villages and up into the mountains. As he began his ascent, he saw an old man carrying a huge bundle on his back, winding his way down the path from the mountains toward him. According to the story, this man was actually the boddhisattva Manjushri who appears

Relief

to people at the moment they are ready for enlightenment.
Greeting the monk, the boddhisattva asked him where he was
heading.

"Oh," said the monk, "I am going to the furthest mountains to find a cave in which to meditate. I will stay there until
I die or realize awakening."

At this point, something made the monk look more closely
at the old man in his path.

"Tell me," he said, "do you know anything of this enlightenment?"

At this point, the old man simply dropped his bundle onto
the ground. Just like that, the monk was enlightened. In an
instant he, too, had put down his whole defensive organiza-
tion, the entire burden. But the newly awakened monk was
still a bit confused.

"Now what?" he asked Manjushri.

And the boddhisattva, smiling, silently reached down,
picked up his bundle, and continued down the path.[8]

Putting down our burdens does not mean forsaking the
conventional world in which our compensatory selves and
thinking minds are necessary, but it means being in that world
with the consciousness of one who is not deceived by appear-
ances. Once Greta had recovered her love for her father, she
could continue to fend him off with forgiveness instead of
rancor. She still needed her defenses, but she was not imprisoned by them. She stopped hating him for imposing so many

restrictions on her expression of love and instead began to work within the limitations without taking them personally. As the newly enlightened monk realized when he saw Manjushri pick up his bundle and head back to town, everything had changed but nothing was altered.

coming home

Of course, this readjustment is fraught with its own share of difficulties, not the least of which is the cockiness that often accompanies a little bit of realization. This point was driven home to me after my last meditation retreat as I was preparing to leave the meditation center and drive myself back to the city. It had begun to snow in the early hours of the morning and had become quite stormy by the time I went out to my automobile after breakfast. I unlocked my car, sat down in the front seat, started up the motor, turned on my headlights, windshield wipers, defroster, and radio, and sat for a moment in the driver's seat, feeling myself reemerge as a confident and capable person. I had a five-hour drive ahead of me through the snowstorm, but I felt clearheaded and well equipped.

I noticed that the snow had caked all over the side and rear windows, and I reached behind me into the backseat to locate the snow brush that lay on the floor. I found and grabbed it without looking, and in one fluid motion I opened my door, pressed the automatic button to "unlock" so that I could get back in, maneuvered myself out of the car, and slammed the door shut to beginning cleaning the windows. I did this all very fast, as if doing a complicated dance that I knew very well, and in an instant I was standing outside my running car with its doors closed, lights on, and windshield wipers and radio going. I knew immediately that something was wrong, however. I had executed my dance perfectly, but with one small mistake. I had locked the door instead of unlocking it and shut myself out of my running car. I had no other key.

My mind was quiet from ten days of meditation, and I could see every thought in Technicolor. I was totally aghast and at the same time slightly amused. I remembered the Sufi Nasruddin, a wise man and fool who was found searching for the key to his house under a lamppost because there was more light there, even though he knew he had lost it elsewhere. I thought briefly of trying that maneuver but realized it was a dead end in this case. I tried every door a couple of times and then trudged up the hill to the meditation center to look for a maintenance person who I thought might have a tool for unlocking the car. I had to wait around for him, but when he finally rolled in, I told him of my predicament.

"I'm sure you've had this happen before," I said hopefully, thinking that he would be able to free me from my situation without further ado.

"Nope," he replied very slowly, elongating each word with the trace of a southern drawl. "Can't say that we have."

I knew then that I would have to call AAA and wait to be rescued. The staff people at the meditation center were doing their best not to make fun of me, but I knew what they were thinking. "Very mindful! Ten days of meditation and he locks his keys in his car."

I went over the seeds of my mistake in my own mind. I was heading back to my real life after the stillness of the meditation retreat. I was invigorated like the old monk who had put down his bundle. There was that moment in the front seat when I thought I could do anything, and I had executed my movements smoothly and efficiently, with such ease. But now I was out in the cold, my car running on without me. "What good was this practice if this is what happens?" I began to think, when suddenly I realized that I was expecting myself, once again, to be infallible. This was another situation in which I was expecting perfection. I was disappointed that the retreat had not yielded up a more efficient and improved self.

"Oh, well," I thought, with the mental equivalent of a sigh, "I might as well learn my lesson right away. I can't even get out the door without stumbling."

But the funny thing was, this is as far as it went. I felt embarrassed but not humiliated. My thoughts did not circle the event endlessly. I adjusted myself to the new reality, waited for half an hour for the AAA man to unlock my door, and in the next instant I was on my way.

I did not need to be infallible to get home, I realized. Nor did I always have to be in control. The retreat *had* changed something in my mind. Retaining a sense of expansiveness toward things instead of the usual contraction, I felt a spirit of generosity toward myself. Things did not have to be perfect for me to be okay, it seemed.

With some gratitude, I realized that my awareness was now stronger than my neurosis. This did not mean that things would never go to pieces, only that I did not have to fall apart when they did. In fact, my own ability to go to pieces was protecting me in this situation. I did not have to let my identity as an efficient and together person imprison me. Rolling through the Massachusetts countryside in the midst of the early morning snowstorm, I felt the freedom that comes from accepting what is. Going down that road, I did not feel half bad.

NOTES

EPIGRAPH

1. John Blofeld, *The Zen Teaching of Huang Po: On the Transmission of Mind* (New York: Grove Press, 1958), p. 41.

INTRODUCTION

1. Paul Reps, *Zen Flesh, Zen Bones* (New York: Anchor Books, 1961), p. 5.

2. See Adam Phillips, *Terrors and Experts* (Cambridge, Mass.: Harvard University Press, 1996), p. 102.

3. Adam Phillips, "Freud and the Uses of Forgetting," in *On Flirtation: Psychoanalytic Essays on the Uncommitted Life* (Cambridge, Mass.: Harvard University Press, 1994), p. 31.

Chapter One: EMPTINESS

1. I have used this story, in a slightly different context, in an article entitled, "Opening Up to Happiness," in *Psychology Today* 28, no. 4 (July/August 1995): pp. 42–47.

2. Lucien Stryck, *World of the Buddha* (New York: Grove Weidenfeld, 1968), pp. 173–74.

3. D. W. Winnicott, *Playing and Reality* (London and New York: Routledge, 1971), p. 55.

4. For theoretical discussions of this kind of experience in therapy, see D. W. Winnicott, "Fear of Breakdown," *International Review of Psycho-Analysis* 1 (1974), and Emmanuel Ghent, "Masochism, Submission, Surrender: Masochism as a Perversion of Surrender," *Contemporary Psychoanalysis* 26:1 (1990): 108–36. Thanks also to Emmanuel Ghent for the suggestion that the *fear* of breakdown also

hides a wish to reexperience that breakdown for the sake of wholeness.

5. I have used this story also in several other contexts, in "Opening Up to Happiness," *Psychology Today* 28, no. 4 (July/August 1995): pp. 42–47, and in "Shattering the Ridgepole," *Tricycle: The Buddhist Review* 4, no. 3 (Spring 1995): pp. 66–70.

6. Joseph Goldstein, *Transforming the Mind, Healing the World* (New York and Mahwah, N.J.: Paulist Press, 1994), pp. 21–23.

7. I have used this vignette in an article entitled "The Silent Treatment," first published in *TimeOut New York*, no. 37 (June 5–12, 1996): pp. 16–18.

Chapter Two: SURRENDER

1. Sigmund Freud, *Civilization and Its Discontents*, in vol. 21 of *Standard Edition of the Complete Works of Sigmund Freud*, ed. and trans. James Strachey (London: Hogarth Press and Institute of Psychoanalysis, 1961), p. 72.

2. See J. Allison, "Adaptive Regression and Intense Religious Experience," *Journal of Nervous and Mental Diseases* 145 (1968): 452–63.

3. Ken Wilber, "The Pre/trans Fallacy," *ReVision* 3 (1980): 58.

4. Tenzin Gyatso, *Kindness, Clarity, and Insight* (Ithaca, N.Y.: Snow Lion, 1984), p. 70.

5. Wallace Stevens, *The Collected Poems of Wallace Stevens* (New York: Vintage Books, 1990), p. 93.

6. D. W. Winnicott, "Communicating and Not Communicating Leading to a Study of Certain Opposites," in *The Maturational Processes and the Facilitating Environment* (New York: International Universities Press, 1965), pp. 185–86.

7. D. W. Winnicott, "Ego Integration in Child Development" (1962), in *The Maturational Processes and the Facilitating Environment*, p. 61.

8. Ibid, pp. 59–60.

9. D. W. Winnicott, "The Capacity to Be Alone" (1958), in *The Maturational Processes and the Facilitating Environment*, p. 31.

10. See Adam Phillips, *Winnicott* (Cambridge, Mass.: Harvard University Press, 1988), pp. 79–82, and Michael Eigen, *The Psychotic Core* (Northvale, N.J.: Jason Aronson Inc., 1986), pp. 331–48 for comprehensive discussions of unintegration.

11. D. W. Winnicott, "Primitive Emotional Development," in *Through Paediatrics to Psycho-Analysis: Collected Papers* (New York: Brunner/Mazel, 1958, 1992), p. 150.

12. See D. W. Winnicott, *Playing and Reality* (London and New York: Routledge, 1971), pp. 79–85.

13. D. W. Winnicott, "Primitive Emotional Development," in *Through Paediatrics to Psycho-Analysis: Collected Papers*, p. 150.

Chapter 3: MEDITATION

1. Paul Goodman, *Five Years: Thoughts During a Useless Time* (New York: Vintage Books, 1966), p. 88.

2. Bhikku Nanamoli and Bhikkhu Bodhi, *The Middle Length Discourses of the Buddha: A New Translation of the Majjhima Nikaya* (Boston: Wisdom Publications, 1995), p. 711.

3. Sigmund Freud, "Inhibitions, Symptoms and Anxiety," in vol. 20 of *Standard Edition of the Complete Psychological Works of Sigmund Freud*, ed. and trans. James Strachey (London: Hogarth Press and Institute of Psychoanalysis, 1959), p. 122.

4. Ibid, p. 121.

5. Ibid, p. 122.

6. Sigmund Freud, "On Transience," in vol. 14 of *Standard Edition of the Complete Psychological Works of Sigmund Freud*, ed. and trans. James Strachey (London: Hogarth Press and Institute of Psychoanalysis, 1957), p. 305.

7. Ibid, pp. 305–6.

8. Philip Kapleau, *The Three Pillars of Zen* (New York, 1966), pp. 297–98, translating from Dogen's *Shobogenzo*.

9. Heinrich Dumoulin, *Zen Buddhism: A History, Volume 1: India and China* (New York: Macmillan Publishing, 1988), p. 163.

10. In Paul Foster, *Beckett and Zen: A Study of Dilemma in the Novels of Samuel Beckett* (London: Wisdom Publications, 1989), p. 93.

Chapter Four: CONNECTION

1. Michael Eigen, *The Psychotic Core* (Northvale, N.J.: Jason Aronson, Inc., 1986), p. 363.

2. Michael Eigen, "Dual Union or Undifferentiation? A Critique of Marion Milner's View of the Sense of Psychic Creativeness," *International Review of Psycho-Analysis* 10 (1983): 424.

3. Stephen Batchelor, *Alone with Others: An Existential Approach to Buddhism* (New York: Grove Weidenfeld, 1983), p. 59.

Chapter Five: TOLERANCE

1. For more on this, see the discussions of Winnicott's notion of "object usage" in Michael Eigen, "The Area of Faith in Winnicott, Lacan and Bion," *International Journal of Psycho-Analysis* 62 (1981): 413–33, and in Emmanuel Ghent, "Masochism, Submission, Surrender: Masochism as a Perversion of Surrender," *Contemporary Psychoanalysis* 26: 1 (1990): 108–36.

2. Gregory Bateson, as quoted in Stephen Nachmanovitch, *Free Play: Improvisation in Life and Art* (Los Angeles: Jeremy P. Tarcher, Inc., 1990), p. 94.

3. Jack Kornfield with Gil Fronsdal, *Teachings of the Buddha* (Boston and London: Shambhala, 1993), p. 85.

4. See in particular D. W. Winnicott, "Mind and Its Relation to the Psyche-Soma," in *Through Paediatrics to Psycho-Analysis* (New York: Brunner/Mazel, 1992), p. 244.

5. For a more extensive discussion of Winnicott's contributions, see Michael Eigen's "Winnicott's Area of Freedom: The Uncompromisable," in *Liminality and Transitional Phenomena*, eds. N. Schwartz-Salant and M. Stein, (Wilmette, Ill.: Chiron Publishers, 1994), and Adam Phillips, "Minds," in his *Terrors and Experts* (Cambridge, Mass.: Harvard University Press, 1996), pp. 93–104.

6. Winnicott, "Mind and Its Relation to the Psyche-Soma," in *Through Paediatrics to Psycho-Analysis*, p. 245.

Chapter Six: RELATIONSHIP

1. D. W. Winnicott, "Playing: A Theoretical Statement," in *Playing and Reality* (London and New York: Routledge, 1971), p. 38.

2. Michael Eigen, "Disaster Anxiety," in *Psychotherapy and the Dangerous Patient*, eds. Jerome A. Travers and E. Mark Stern (Binghamton, NY: The Haworth Press, 1994), p. 62.

3. See Stephen Batchelor, *Buddhism Without Beliefs: A Contemporary Guide to Awakening* (New York: Riverhead Books, 1997), p. 105, and also his *The Faith to Doubt: Glimpses of Buddhist Uncertainty* (Berkeley, Calif.: Parallax Press, 1990).

4. See Miranda Shaw's *Passionate Enlightenment* (Princeton, N.J.: Princeton University Press, 1994), p. 22.

Chapter Seven: PASSION

1. Roland Barthes, *A Lover's Discourse: Fragments* (New York: Hill and Wang, 1978), p. 137.

2. Robert A. F. Thurman, "Mandala: The Architecture of Enlightenment," in *Mandala: The Architecture of Enlightenment*, eds. Denise P. Leidy and Robert A. F. Thurman (Boston: Shambhala, 1997), p. 127.

3. Christopher Bollas, *The Shadow of the Object: Psychoanalysis of the Unthought Known* (New York: Columbia University Press, 1987), p. 31.

4. See for instance, Jeffrey Hopkins, *Tibetan Arts of Love: Sex, Orgasm and Spiritual Healing* (Ithaca, N.Y.: Snow Lion, 1992), and Miranda Shaw, *Passionate Enlightenment* (Princeton, N.J.: Princeton University Press, 1994).

5. Miranda Shaw, *Passionate Enlightenment*, p. 163.

6. Ibid, p. 158.

7. See Richard Jay Kohn, "The Goddess Who Stands at the Door: Sorceresses and Other Liminal Figures in Tibetan Iconography," presented in "Politics and Religion in Nepal and Tibet," American Academy of Religion, San Francisco, November 22, 1992.

8. Otto Kernberg, *Love Relations: Normality and Pathology* (New Haven, Conn.: Yale University Press, 1995), p. 61.

9. Ibid, p. 57.

10. Ibid, p. 44.

11. Michael Vincent Miller, *Intimate Terrorism: The Deterioration of Erotic Life* (New York and London: W. W. Norton, 1995), p. 229.

12. See Stephen A. Mitchell, "Psychoanalysis and the Degradation of Romance," *Psychoanalytic Dialogues* 7, no. 1 (1997): 23–42.

Chapter Eight: RELIEF

1. See E. A. Burtt, ed., *The Teachings of the Compassionate Buddha* (New York: Mentor Books, 1955), pp. 98–100.

2. From the *Majjhima Nikaya*, trans. Nyanatiloka, *The Word of the Buddha* (Kandy, Sri Lanka: Buddhist Publication Society, 1971).

3. See Herbert Benson, John Lehmann, Mahendra Malhotra, Ralph Goldman, Jeffrey Hopkins, and Mark Epstein, "Body Temperature Changes During the Practice of gTum-mo Yoga," *Nature* 295 (1982): 234–6.

4. For more extensive discussions of these practices, see the reports of our translator on this research expedition, Jeffrey Hopkins in his *Tibetan Arts of Love: Sex, Orgasm and Spiritual Healing* (Ithaca, N.Y.: Snow Lion, 1992), pp. 95–120, and his *Sex, Orgasm, and the Mind of Clear Light: The Sixty-Four Arts of Gay Male Love* (Berkeley, Calif.: North Atlantic Press, 1998).

See also Tenzin Gyatso, the Dalai Lama, and Jeffrey Hopkins, *Kalachakra Tantra Rite of Initiation* (London: Wisdom Publications, 1985), pp. 15–18.

5. Heinz Pagels, *The Cosmic Code* (New York: Bantam Books, 1983).

6. See Tulku Urgyen Rinpoche, *Rainbow Painting* (Boudhanath and Hong Kong: Rangjung Yeshe Publications, 1995).

7. See Jeffrey Hopkins, *Sex, Orgasm, and the Mind of Clear Light:*

The Sixty-Four Arts of Gay Male Love (Berkeley, Calif.: North Atlantic Press, 1998).

8. See Joseph Goldstein and Jack Kornfield, *Seeking the Heart of Wisdom: The Path of Insight Meditation* (Boston and London: Shambhala, 1987), pp. 168–69.

INDEX

A

Abenaki Indian story of stopping the wind, 129–130
activating the imagination in psychotherapy (case example), 133–134
adulthood, tasks of, 47–48
advanced meditation practices, 164–167
aging
  fear of, 161–164
  Nakulapita and aging story, 159–160
aloneness, sense of, 38–39
Alpert, Richard, 75–79
ambition interfering with success, 51–53

anger
  as self-liberating, 130
  transforming to desire (case example), 149–155, 157–158
Angulimala (bandit) story, 56–57
Anguttara Nikaya, 102–103
anticipating the past as obstacle to unintegration, 43
anvil metaphor for emptiness, 13–14
artifice versus naturalness, 91–92
attachment and aversion, 61–64

B

Batchelor, Stephen, activating the imagination in psychotherapy (case example), 133–134

bathroom door metaphor for
relaxing boundaries of ego,
87–88
being. *See* learning to be
"being-time" (Dogen), 65–66
Benson, Herbert, advanced
meditation practices, study of,
164–167
body
freeing from mind, 159–160
mindfulness of, 106–108
Gestalt therapy (case example),
121–124
mindfulness of feelings, 108–110
breathing in meditation (case
example), 80–82
Buddha's teachings
achieving enlightenment and
touching earth, 117–118
delusion, 125–126
"Four Foundations of
Mindfulness," 105–106
body, 106–108
feelings, 108–110
mind, 112–113
thoughts and emotions, 110–
112
happiness and aging, 159–160
mind as nugget of gold, 168–169
separateness, coming to terms
with, 118
three messengers metaphor, 163–
164
transience, 64–66
Buddhism
authenticating feelings of
emptiness, 124–125
connections, 55–56
individuals as overlapping
environments, 135
integrating feelings to achieve
wholeness, 102
links with psychotherapy, 12–16

mind
location and meaning of,
106
way of working with, 19–20
moments of unknowing, 46
Buddhist path and meditation, 70
Buddhist sutra, Anguttara Nikaya,
102–103
Buddhist versus Western
perspective
birth and individuality, 85–86
connection, 75
emptiness, 13–16
feminine versus masculine, 86–
87
mind, 112–113
self relaxing its boundaries, 84–
86
unconscious, 86–87
view of growth and
development, 83–85
view of self, 35–36

C
capacity to be, 39–41
case example, 42–45
insufficient development (case
example), 88–90
capacity to be alone, paradox of,
38–39
clear light nature of mind
accessing, 168–170
case example, 171–173
as foundation of healing, 170–
171
positive emptiness, 160–161
connections
being versus doing, 90–92
Buddhist perspective, 55–56
embracing impermanence to
permit, 70–72
isolating self with obsessive
thinking, 57–61

mind interfering with ability to make contact (case example), 54–55

Ram Dass interview, 75–79

reason for seeking therapy, 73–75

surrendering ego to feel, 87

D

Dalai Lama, search for happiness, meeting with, xvii, 165–166

death
  fear of, 161–164
    son clinging story, 96–98
  and impermanence in Kisagotami and the mustard seed story, 6–9
  meditation as practice for, 164–167
  Tibetan master's son story, 64

defense
  definition, 127
  reappraising in psychotherapy (case example), 173–176, 177–178

delusion, definition, 125–126

desire, transforming anger to (case example), 149–155, 157–158

differences, respecting in relationships, 155–156

disappointments in relationships, 143–144
  converting to empathy, 156–157
  transforming passion (case example), 149–155, 157–158

Dogen and "being-time," 65–66

doing versus being, 90–92

E

ego
  healing effects of loss of, 31–33
  maintaining control, 81–82
  as necessary fiction, 87

perpetuating hold of, 51–53

relaxing boundaries
  case example, 88–90
  metaphor of bathroom door, 87–88

surrendering in meditation, 69–70

transcendence versus regression, 32–34

See also self

Eigen, Michael
  intimacy and aloneness, 74
  merger and isolation, 84
  using meditation to control others (case example), 128–129, 131

Eightfold Path, 118

emotions
  learning to be with in new ways, 131–133
  mindfulness of, 110–112
  staying with emotional states, 22–24
  emptiness, 26–27
  See also feeling states

empathy
  converting disappointments to in relationships, 156–157
  generating capacity for, 113

emptiness, sense of
  anvil metaphor, 13–14
  authenticating feelings of, 124–125
  Buddhist perspective, 13–14
  cultivating spiritual maturity from, 6–9
  fears
    dealing with in psychotherapy, 20–24
    fragility of bond with parent, 18–19
  interpreting in psychotherapy, 5–6, 14–16

Kernberg, Otto, 10–12
learning to bear, 22–25
  ritual harmonic chanting
    analogy, 26–27
  meditation, 16–17
  mirroring in psychotherapy, 9–
    10
  positive, the clear light nature of
    mind, 160–161
  rabbi and breaking wine glass
    story, 70–71, 72
  transforming, 16
  universal experience, 3–4
enlightenment
  Buddha achieving and touching
    earth, 117–118
  Manibhadra, story of, 134–135
expectations
  disappointments in relationships,
    143–144
  converting to empathy, 156–
    157
  transforming passion (case
    example), 149–155, 157–158
  of perfection, interfering with
    what is, 114–116
  self as infallible (case example),
    178–181

F

fears
  aging, illness, and death, 161–
    164
  son clinging story, 96–98
  being overwhelmed by emotions,
    111
  emptiness, 14–16
    dealing with in psychotherapy,
      20–24
    fragility of bond with parent,
      18–19
  falling apart, xviii–xix
  feelings, 98–100

giving up control and breathing
    meditation, 81–82
  separateness in relationships,
    143–144
feeling states
  anger as self-liberating, 130
  crossing human boundaries, 95–
    96
  mindfulness of, 108–110
  surviving, 99–101
  unacknowledged, 103
    case example, 104–105
  unawareness of, 98–100
  See also emotions
feminine versus masculine traits,
    86–87
Ferenczi, Sándor, xix–xx
"Four Foundations of
    Mindfulness," 105–106
  body, 106–108
  feelings, 108–110
  Gestalt therapy (case example),
    121–124
  mind, 112–113
  thoughts and emotions, 110–112
free-associating, xix–xx
freedom from the known, 45–46
Freud, Sigmund
  "On Transience," 61–64
  unconscious and feeling states,
    95–96
From, Isadore, 91–92
fundamental unreality of the self,
    34–36

G

Gestalt therapy (case example),
    121–124
goddesses on Nepalese shrine, 148–
    149
growth and development as linear,
    83–85

Index

H

happiness, Buddhist way to
    achieve, xv–xviii
healing
    definition, 106
    foundation of, 170–173
"heat yoga" practices, 166–167
holding environment
    creating, 37–39
    good enough, 113–114

I

illness, fear of, 161–164
imagination, activating in
    psychotherapy (case example),
    133–134
impermanence, embracing, 70–72
inauthenticity as obstacle to love,
    74–75
individuals as overlapping
    environments, 135
interconnectedness with world,
    117–118
interpreting
    emptiness, 5–6
    problems with approach, 14–
    16
    feelings, 99–100
involuntary nervous system,
    meditation practices to
    control, 166–167
isolating self with obsessive
    thinking, 57–61

J

juggling and not being in the mind
    (case example), 29–31
Jungian therapy, "Sandplay" (case
    example), 133–134

K

karma, definition, 86
Kernberg, Otto, 10–12
    sexual intimacy, 151, 155

Kisagotami and the mustard seed
    story, 6–9
koan practice, 24–25
Kohn, Richard, and Nepalese
    shrine, 148–149
Kris, Ernst, "regression in the
    service of the ego," 32–33

L

Lacan, Jacques, delusion, 126
learning to be
    being versus doing, 90–92
    meditating to restore balance
        between doing and being, 80–
        82
    Ram Dass interview, 75–79
leaving alone, 17–19
love
    obstacle to, 74–75
    permitting versus doing or
        feeling, 80
    separateness and connection, 78–
        79
luminous nature of mind. *See* clear
    light nature of mind

M

Mahler, Margaret, separation/
    individuation, 83–85
mandala
    description of, 141
    enlightening experience, 144
    entering, 143
    meaning of, 141–142
    Nepalese shrine constructed as,
        148–149
    principles of, 150–151
    using sexual imagery, 147–148
Manibhadra and enlightenment
    story, 134–135
Manjushri (boddhisattva) story of
    realization, 176–177
Ma-tsu (monk) story, 68–69

meditation
in action, 127–128
renunciation, 140–141
advanced practices, 164–167
bringing awareness to everyday
life, 131
Buddhist path and, 70
comparing joy of to falling in
love, xx–xxi
encouraging development of
trust, 90
four postures for awareness of
body, 107–108
getting the mind out of the
way
Angulimala (bandit) story, 56–
57
"soft eyes" metaphor, 51–53
stammering analogy, 53–54
healing (definition), 106
koan practice, 24–25
Ma-tsu (monk) story, 68–69
mindfulness or bare attention
technique, 67–68
mountains and rivers metaphor,
139–141
passions and emotions, 149
as practice for death, 164–167
preparing ground for intimacy,
75
repetitive thinking, 59–61
restoring balance between doing
and being, 80–82
revealing early traumas, 109–110
sense of emptiness, 5–6, 16–17
versus sexual tantras, 147
spiritual path, progress on, 120–
121
surrendering ego and mind, 69–
70
taming of the heart, 102–104
transforming obstacles into
objects of, 130

using to control others (case
example), 128–129, 131
watcher putting worry and self-
consciousness on hold, 66–67
watching breathing (case
example), 80–82
Miller, Michael Vincent
Gestalt therapy (case example),
121–124
Intimate Terrorism, 156–157
mind
Buddhist way of working with,
19–20
clear light nature of
accessing, 168–170
case example, 171–173
as foundation of healing, 170–
171
positive emptiness, 160–161
cultivating, 61–64
freeing from body, 159–161
getting it out of the way
Angulimala (bandit) story, 56–
57
"soft eyes" metaphor, 51–53
stammering analogy, 53–54
interfering with ability to
connect (case example),
54–55
location and meaning of in
Buddhism, 106
mindfulness of, 112–113
as nugget of gold, 168–169
vigilance of
preventing connections, 58–61
relaxing, 47–48
wind as metaphor for, 129–130
mindfulness meditation, 67–68
body, 106–108
Gestalt therapy (case example),
121–124
feelings, 108–110
mind, 112–113

taming of the heart, 102–104
thoughts and emotions, 110–112
mirroring technique, 9–10
mother's tasks
  holding environment, creating,
    37–39
  interpreting and surviving
    emotions, 99–100
  leaving child alone, 17–19
mountains and rivers metaphor,
  139–141
mourning
  fending off inevitable, 63–64
  protecting self from, 65–66
mustard seed and Kisagotami story,
  6–9

N
Nakulapita and aging story, 159–
  160
naturalness versus artifice, 91–92
Nepalese shrine and goddesses,
  148–149

O
orgasm as window to mind of pure
  being, 142
original union (mother and infant),
  belief in, 83–85
  dark side of, 86–87
overflowing cup story, xv–xvi, xxi

P
Pagels, Heinz, mind that dawns in
  death, 167–168
passions, transforming, 147–148
path. See spiritual path
patients unaware of feeling states,
  98–100
perfection
  expectations of
    interfering with what is (case
      example), 114–116

self as infallible (case example),
  178–181
transforming anger to desire
  (case example), 149–155, 157–
  158
of parents, 113
surrendering ideas of, xviii
playing
  "the box" technique, 96–98
  Winnicott, D. W., 126–127
"pre/trans fallacy" (Ken Wilber),
  33–34
projective identification, 95–96
psychoanalysis
  emotional experience, origins of,
    99–100
  healing effects of loss of ego,
    31–33
  Kernberg, Otto, and emptiness,
    10–12
psychological materialism, xvi
search for happiness, xvii–xviii
psychotherapy
  activating the imagination (case
    example), 133–134
  analysis of childhood, xix–xx
  comparing to meditation, xix–xx
  defense, 127
  defensive nature of thinking, 60–
    61
  developing the self, xviii–xx
  fear of emptiness (case example),
    20–24
  Gestalt therapy (case example),
    121–124
  integrating feelings for
    wholeness, 102
  interpreting sense of emptiness,
    5–6
  links with Buddhism, 12–16
  mirroring technique, 9–10
  playing, 126–127

reappraisal in (case example),
173–176, 177–178
reasons for seeking, 73–74
reestablishing capacity to be, 41
    case example, 42–45
restoring capacity for emotional
    experience (case example),
    131–133
targeting fear of emptiness, 16–
    17
treating emptiness, 15–16
window to absence of
    identification, 170–171
putting down burdens, 176–178

R
rabbi breaking wine glass story,
    70–71, 72
Ram Dass, interview with, 75–79
realization
    case example, 178–181
    story of Manjushri (boddhisatva),
        176–177
"regression in the service of the
    ego" (Ernst Kris), 32–33
regression versus transcendence,
    33–34
relationships
    converting disappointments to
        empathy, 156–157
    discovering capacities for, 120
    respecting differences, 155–156
    transforming anger to desire
        (case example), 149–155, 157–
        158
relaxing boundaries of ego
    case example, 88–90
    metaphor of bathroom door, 87–
        88
relaxing into the truth, 20
renunciation, 140–141
Rinpoche, definition, 13

ritual harmonic chanting analogy,
    26–27

S
"Sandplay," Jungian therapy (case
    example), 133–134
self
    building a path through, 118–
        120
    building out of defenses, 176
    compensatory selves, 177–178
    dropping oppressive feeling of,
        21–22
    expecting infallibility (case
        example), 178–181
    freeing mind from body, 159–
        161
    fundamental unreality of, 34–36
    getting out of the way for
        connections, 55–56
    healing effects of loss of ego,
        31–33
    isolating with obsessive thinking,
        57–61
    letting go of, 45–47
    mirroring, importance of, 9–10
    permeability of, 84–86
    psychotherapy and development
        of, xviii–xx
    Western psychology view of, xv–
        xvi
    See also ego
sense of aloneness, 38–39
sense of emptiness
    authenticating feelings of, 124–
        125
    Buddhist perspective, 13–14
    cultivating spiritual maturity
        from, 6–9
    fears
        dealing with in psychotherapy,
            20–24

fragility of bond with parent, 18–19

interpreting in psychotherapy, 5–6

Kernberg, Otto, 10–12

learning to bear, 22–25
 ritual harmonic chanting analogy, 26–27

meditation, 16–17

mirroring in psychotherapy, 9–10

rabbi breaking wine glass story, 70–71, 72

transforming, 16

universal experience, 3–4

separateness
 coming to terms with, 118
 converting disappointments to empathy, 156–157
 fearing relationships, 143–144
 mountains and rivers metaphor, 139–141
 tolerating in mature sexual relationships, 155

separation
 and connectedness, 78–79
 /individuation (Margaret Mahler), 83–85
 sexual relations, 144–145
 Kernberg, Otto, 151, 155
 sexual tantra, 145–147

shoulder tension story (juggling and not being in the mind), 29–31

"soft eyes" metaphor, 51–53

spirituality and sexual relations, 145–147

spiritual maturity, cultivating from sense of emptiness, 6–9

spiritual path
 making, 118–120
 meditation and progress on, 120–121

stammering story (getting the mind out of the way), 53–54

staying with an emotional state, 22–24
 emptiness, 26–27

Stein, Robbie, 96

stopping the wind story, 129–130

surviving (child's) emotions, 99–100

T

"tamed heart," 102–104
 case example, 104–105

thinking as interfering with connecting, 58–61

thoughts
 mindfulness of, 110–112
 as weeds metaphor, 112

three messengers metaphor, 163–164

Tibetan Book of the Dead, 169

Tibetan Buddhist perspective
 sexual relations, 144–145
 sexual tantra, 145–147

tolerance
 disappointments in relationships, 143–144
 for feelings
  exchanging with others to facilitate, 100–101
  paradox of, 102
 generating capacity for empathy, 113
 inherent capacity of mind for, 114
 of separateness in mature sexual relationships, 155

transcendence versus regression, 32–34

transforming
 anger to desire (case example), 149–155, 157–158
 experience of emptiness, 16

obstacles into objects of
    meditation, 130
passions, 147–148
transience
    Buddha's teachings on, 64–66
    death of Tibetan master's son
        story, 64
    embracing, 70–72
    inability to appreciate, 61–64
traumas, uncovering early in
    meditation, 109–110
trust, encouraging development of
    through meditation, 90

U
unacknowledged feeling states, 103
    case example, 104–105
unawareness of feeling states, 98–
    100
unconscious (Freudian), 86–87
unintegration
    anticipating past as obstacle to,
        43
    capacity to be, 39–41
        case example, 42–45
    definition, 36–37
    versus disintegration, 47–48
    holding environment, creating,
        37–39
    integrating feelings for
        wholeness, 102
universal experiences
    death and impermanence, 6–9
    sense of emptiness, 3–4

W
watching breathing in meditation
    (case example), 80–82
Western versus Buddhist
    perspective
    emptiness, 13–16
    feminine versus masculine, 86–
        87
    material and psychological
        acquisitiveness, xvi
    mind, 112–113
    unconscious, 86–87
    view of growth and
        development, 83–85
    view of self, 35–36, xv-xvi
Wilber, Ken, "pre/trans fallacy,"
    33–34
wind, Buddhist metaphor for
    mind, 129–130
Winnicott, D. W.
    delusion, 126
    "feeling real," 15–16
    "good-enough ego coverage,"
        17–20
    good enough parents, 113
    playing, 126–127
    unintegration
        capacity to be, 39–41
        experiencing, 36–39

Z
Zen master and overflowing cup
    story, xv-xvi, xxi